REGENTS RESTORATION DR

General Editor: John Loftis

A BOLD STROKE FOR A WIFE

SUSANNA CENTLIVRE

A Bold Stroke for a Wife

Edited by

THALIA STATHAS

UNIVERSITY OF NEBRASKA PRESS · LINCOLN

Regents Restoration Drama Series

The Regents Restoration Drama Series provides soundly edited texts, in modern spelling, of the more significant plays of the late seventeenth and early eighteenth centuries. The word "Restoration" is here used ambiguously and must be explained. If to the historian it refers to the period between 1660 and 1685 (or 1688), it has long been used by the student of drama in default of a more precise word to refer to plays belonging to the dramatic tradition established in the 1660's, weakening after 1700, and displaced in the 1730's. It is in this extended sense—imprecise though justified by academic custom—that the word is used in this series, which includes plays first produced between 1660 and 1737. Although these limiting dates are determined by political events, the return of Charles II (and the removal of prohibitions against operation of theaters) and the passage of Walpole's Stage Licensing Act, they enclose a period of dramatic history having a coherence of its own in the establishment, development, and disintegration of a tradition.

Some fifteen editions having appeared as this volume goes to press, the series has reached perhaps a third of its anticipated range of between forty and fifty volumes. The volumes will continue to be published for a number of years, at the rate of three or more annually. From the beginning the editors have planned the series with attention to the projected dimensions of the completed whole, a representative collection of Restoration drama providing a record of artistic achievement and providing also a record of the deepest concerns of three generations of Englishmen. And thus it contains deservedly famous plays—*The Country Wife*, *The Man of Mode*, and *The Way of the World*—and also significant but little known plays, *The Virtuoso*, for example, and *City Politiques*, the former a satirical review of scientific investigation in the early years of the Royal Society, the latter an equally satirical review of politics at the time of the Popish Plot. If the volumes of famous plays finally achieve the larger circulation, the other volumes may conceivably have the greater utility, in making available texts otherwise difficult of access with the editorial apparatus needed to make them intelligible.

The editors have had the instructive example of the parallel and senior project, the Regents Renaissance Drama Series; they have in fact used the editorial policies developed for the earlier plays as their own, modifying them as appropriate for the later period and as the experience of successive editions suggested. The introductions to the separate Restoration plays differ considerably in their nature. Although a uniform body of relevant information is presented in each of them, no attempt has been made to impose a pattern of interpretation. Emphasis in the introductions has necessarily varied with the nature of the plays and inevitably—we think desirably—with the special interests and aptitudes of the different editors.

Each text in the series is based on a fresh collation of the seventeenth- and eighteenth-century editions that might be presumed to have authority. The textual notes, which appear above the rule at the bottom of each page, record all substantive departures from the edition used as the copy-text. Variant substantive readings among contemporary editions are listed there as well. Editions later than the eighteenth century are referred to in the textual notes only when an emendation originating in some one of them is received into the text. Variants of accidentals (spelling, punctuation, capitalization) are not recorded in the notes. Contracted forms of characters' names are silently expanded in speech prefixes and stage directions, and, in the case of speech prefixes, are regularized. Additions to the stage directions of the copy-text are enclosed in brackets.

Spelling has been modernized along consciously conservative lines, but within the limits of a modernized text the linguistic quality of the original has been carefully preserved. Contracted preterites have regularly been expanded. Punctuation has been brought into accord with modern practice. The objective has been to achieve a balance between the pointing of the old editions and a system of punctuation which, without overloading the text with exclamation marks, semicolons, and dashes, will make the often loosely flowing verse and prose of the original syntactically intelligible to the modern reader. Dashes are regularly used only to indicate interrupted speeches, or shifts of address within a single speech.

Explanatory notes, chiefly concerned with glossing obsolete words and phrases, are printed below the textual notes at the bottom of each page. References to stage directions in the notes follow the admirable system of the Revels editions, whereby stage directions are keyed, decimally, to the line of the text before or after which they occur. Thus, a note on 0.2 has reference to the second line of the stage direction at the beginning of the scene in question. A note on 115.1 has reference to the first line of the stage direction following line 115 of the text of the relevant scene. Speech prefixes, and any stage directions attached to them, are keyed to the first line of accompanying dialogue.

JOHN LOFTIS

October, 1967
Stanford University

Contents

List of Abbreviations

arch.   archaic

Bowyer   John Wilson Bowyer. *The Celebrated Mrs. Centlivre.* Durham, N.C., 1952.

D1   First edition, 12*mo.*, 1718.

D1a   First edition, British Museum copy.

D1b   First edition, Bodleian and Harvard copies.

D2   "Second Edition," 12*mo.*, 1724.

fig.   figurative

ME   Middle English

obs.   obsolete

OED   *Oxford English Dictionary*

S.D.   stage direction

S.P.   speech prefix

Introduction

First performed in February, 1718, *A Bold Stroke for a Wife*, "*By the Author of the* Busie-Body *and the* Gamester," was published that year, probably in the same month, by "*W. Mears, J. Browne,* and *F. Clay.*"[1] William Mears was the principal partner in most early editions of Mrs. Centlivre's comedy. Publisher as well for Defoe, Dennis, Philips, and Theobald, he aroused Pope's wrath and appears in *The Dunciad* (A, III.20; B, III.28). In 1719, he assembled *A Collection of Plays By Eminent Hands,* including *A Bold Stroke for a Wife* in Volume III. Mears used pages left over from the first edition, retaining the original preliminaries. Since, at the most, he prefixed a half-title page to them, this printing is better termed a first edition than a new issue.[2] With Clay he published the second edition in 1724, the year after Mrs. Centlivre's death.[3] In 1728, Thomas Astley reissued it in London, replacing the original title page with a new one which bears only his imprint. The year before, a Dublin edition based on the second had appeared, and in 1729, the third London edition followed, again from the presses of Mears and Clay.[4]

Of the early editions, only the first two can claim authority; it is in

[1] An advertisement in *The Daily Courant* for February 28, 1718, announces the publication of the comedy.

[2] As the discussion of the first edition will also suggest, it is questionable whether the half-title appeared in 1718 or was added in 1719. Insofar as I have been able to determine, it is not conjugate with any other page in the first edition. In the copies of the half-title examined, the water mark is missing. The stock appears to be similar, but not identical, to that of the preliminaries and text.

[3] Biographical problems and information regarding Mrs. Centlivre are discussed in the following works: James R. Sutherland, "The Progress of Error: Mrs. Centlivre and the Biographers," *Review of English Studies,* XVIII (1942), 167–182; John Wilson Bowyer, *The Celebrated Mrs. Centlivre* (Durham, N.C., 1952); and John H. MacKenzie, "Susan Centlivre," *Notes and Queries,* CXCVIII (1953), 386–390.

[4] Bowyer has examined seventeen eighteenth-century printings and editions of *A Bold Stroke for a Wife* and eighteen nineteenth-century ones (p. 217). The play has not previously been printed in the twentieth century.

fact doubtful that Mrs. Centlivre prepared the second. In both of its states, copies of the first edition (D1) are rare. Three have been collated for this edition. The copy-text is a separately bound duodecimo in the Bodleian Library; gathered in sixes, it was probably imposed by half-sheet.[5] The other copies are in the British Museum and the Harvard College Library. A duodecimo second edition in the library of the University of London (D2) has also been collated.[6] The British Museum's copy of D1 appears in *A Collection of Plays By Eminent Hands*; Harvard's is separately bound. The Bodleian's may once have formed part of the *Collection*, for the recto of a page facing the title page is identical to the half-title probably added in 1719. Harvard's copy lacks this page altogether. It has been trimmed so closely at the top that its headlines are mutilated and the first word (*A*) is missing from the title page.

Except for these defects, Harvard's copy of D1 corresponds exactly with the Bodleian's, which is perfect. The British Museum's, also perfect, contains three press variants, all in the fifth signed gathering, on [E3v] and [E4]. Only one of them is substantive;[7] it occurs in IV.iii.91, of the present edition. The British Museum's copy reads, "*Fortune reward the faithful Lover's Pain.*" The other copies use the third person singular, *rewards*, rather than the imperative. Spacing of type in these readings suggests that the press was stopped for alteration after the British Museum's copy was printed. Therefore, to indicate

[5] Allardyce Nicoll describes the first edition as an octavo, dated 1718; he refers to a duodecimo of 1719, making no mention of a 1718 duodecimo (*A History of English Drama: 1660–1900* [Cambridge, England, 1952], II, 305). The first edition cited by *The Cambridge Bibliography of English Literature* is that of 1718, appearing in Mears's *Collection* (II, 433). Although unable to trace an octavo first edition, Miss J. E. Norton questions whether the 1718 edition by Mears, Browne, and Clay is the first because it appears to start "part way through a gathering" ("Some Uncollected Authors XIV: Susanna Centlivre," *Book Collector*, VI [1957], 177): [–]2, A–F6, G2. In fact, the preliminaries have undoubtedly been printed on the same sheet with G2, for both of these gatherings have vertical chain lines; those in A–F6 are horizontal. Probably for economy or because of a shortage of stock, an odd-sized partial sheet was used to print the preliminaries and G2, after the rest of the text had been printed.

[6] This copy is bound in *The English Theatre. Part II* (London, 1731), VI.

[7] [E3v] and [E4] belong to the same forme; once the press had been stopped for the substantive change, one punctuational and one typographical change were also made. SCENE was changed to *SCENE*; and a semicolon was substituted for a comma after *Body* in what is IV.iii.77, of the present edition.

the sequence of variant copies here, the siglum D1a has been assigned to the British Museum's and D1b to Harvard's and the Bodleian's. Both readings are equally logical in context. The present edition accepts *rewards*, as do D2, all other editions through 1729, and that in the first collection of Mrs. Centlivre's dramatic works (W).[8] Since the compositor did not alter readings elsewhere, it seems unlikely that he would have stopped the press here, had *reward* not departed from the copy being set. Presumably it bore the dramatist's authority.

D2 follows D1 closely, introducing only occasional substantive variants. Sometimes it corrects an obvious mistake in D1 or clearly errs itself. Significant errors and all substantive variants in both editions have been recorded as they occur, in textual notes, as have significant punctuational variants and emendations of the copy-text. D1 has been emended with caution; whenever it has been altered, D2's reading has been adopted if it is suitable; all other editions through 1729 and W have also been consulted. Save for the exceptions already described, punctuation and spelling have been silently modernized. Contractions lacking phonetic significance in the early eighteenth century have been expanded without mention; for example, *shou'd* and *wou'd* have been emended to *should* and *would*. All other contractions have been allowed to stand. Although French spelling has been silently modernized, Dutch has not been brought into accord with modern usage; for to so edit it would destroy the author's humorous, phonetically conceived Dutch-English hybrids.

A Bold Stroke for a Wife was first produced at Lincoln's Inn Fields on February 3, 1718.[9] It was performed six times, almost consecutively, with Christopher Bullock playing Fainwell, the comedy's most demanding part. Despite initial success, it was not performed again until 1724, and then not in London but on Epsom Walks by a company of strolling actors.[10] Lincoln's Inn Fields revived the play, "Not Acted these Ten Years," on April 23, 1728, with Milward as Fainwell. For the next decade, it was staged in London principally

8 *The Works of the Celebrated Mrs. Centlivre. . . . With a New Account of her Life* (London, 1760,1761), 3 vols.; *A Bold Stroke for a Wife* appears in Volume III.

9 Unless otherwise noted, information regarding the play's stage history is based on Parts II, III, and IV of *The London Stage: 1660–1800*, ed. Emmett L. Avery, *et al.* (Carbondale, Ill., 1960–).

10 Bowyer, p. 215.

under Henry Giffard's management, at Goodman's Fields and then at Lincoln's Inn Fields. Unlike managers at the other theaters, he favored contemporary and recent works over those of the Restoration;[11] he frequently staged *A Bold Stroke for a Wife*, *The Wonder* (1714), and *The Busy Body* (1709), Mrs. Centlivre's most popular comedies. In *A Bold Stroke for a Wife*, Giffard presented such distinguished comedians as Huddy, Pinkethman, Bullock, Sr., and Norris. Often he produced the comedy with supplementary entertainments, ranging from dancing and singing to operas and other plays.

In the 1730's, *A Bold Stroke for a Wife* was also staged by Covent Garden, Drury Lane, the new theater in the Haymarket, and the theater at Southwark. On the Kentish circuit, Dymer's company played it at Margate in 1730.[12] In London, Mrs. Clive led the first cast at Drury Lane on January 13, 1739, with Milward as Fainwell and Woodward as Simon Pure. She was the most distinguished actress to take the role of Ann Lovely; at other London theaters, it had most often been played by Mrs. Berriman, Mrs. Hamilton, Mrs. Haughton, and Mrs. Younger. A new part was, apparently, added at Drury Lane, for cast listings regularly include Mrs. "Pickup," a role also listed by Goodman's Fields for a performance on October 16, 1741.[13]

During 1740 and 1741, Drury Lane continued to produce *A Bold Stroke for a Wife*, once "By His Majesty's Command" (March 5, 1741). Nevertheless, in the 1740's, the play's stage history is dominated by Goodman's Fields, where it was produced fifteen times between October, 1740, and March, 1747. The management evaded the Licensing Act by presenting it "gratis" during intermissions at concerts or with tumbling and dancing.[14] In this same period, theatrical booths at the fairs produced the comedy as a two-act droll, *The Guardians over-reached in their Own Humour: or, the Lover Metamorphos'd*.[15] In the provinces, a company visiting Ipswich staged the

[11] See Arthur H. Scouten, *The London Stage: 1660–1800, Part Three: 1729–1747* (Carbondale, Ill., 1961), I, lxxxii.

[12] Sybil Rosenfeld, *Strolling Players and Drama in the Provinces, 1660–1765* (Cambridge, England, 1939), p. 221.

[13] I have not been able to determine the nature of this role or whether a printed text including it exists.

[14] See *The London Stage: 1660–1800, Part Three: 1729–1747*, II, the entry for Goodman's Fields, April 16, 1745.

[15] Bowyer, p. 216. This version of the play is included in *The Stroller's Pacquet Open'd* (London, 1742); the title page of the droll is dated 1741.

play in January, 1741, and the Bristol company performed it in 1745.[16]

By the middle of the century, *A Bold Stroke for a Wife* had been staged about eighty times in London theaters. Yet, as with *The Wonder*, one of Garrick's favorite plays, this comedy's greatest popularity came after 1750. During the season of 1757–1758, Edward Shuter first played Fainwell at Covent Garden; by 1762, he had performed this part almost as often as Garrick had Don Felix, in *The Wonder*, at Drury Lane. Having earlier diverted audiences as Periwinkle, Shuter decided to attempt Fainwell in a benefit for himself on April 3, 1758. His advertisement of March 8 suggests the reasons for his choice: "Mrs. Centlivre's Comedies have a vein of pleasantry in them that will always be relish'd. She knew the Genius of this nation, and she wrote up to the spirit of it; her *Bold Stroke for a Wife*, was a masterpiece that much increased her reputation: it establish'd that of Kit Bullock . . . ."[17] Shuter's choice proved sound; the receipts for his benefit were the largest of the season.[18]

In 1762, Henry Woodward returned to London theater after an absence of several seasons. Thereafter, for more than a decade at Covent Garden, he appeared as Fainwell and Shuter as Periwinkle or Prim. During the last part of the century, the play continued to be produced, averaging six performances each year.[19] John Philip Kemble staged it often because of its reliability in pleasing his audiences. The comedy remained popular in the nineteenth century, when Charles Kemble, Charles Mathews, and Robert Elliston appeared in it, enhancing its reputation as an acting play. With these performers the stage history of *A Bold Stroke for a Wife* came to a close. No major company has produced it during the twentieth century; however, in a performance at Ealing in 1954, Questor's Theatre demonstrated that this comedy is still effective upon the boards.[20]

[16] Rosenfeld, pp. 99, 207.

[17] *The Public Advertiser;* quoted in *The London Stage: 1660–1800, Part Four: 1747–1776*, ed. George Winchester Stone, Jr. (Carbondale, Ill., 1962), II, the entry for April 3, 1758.

[18] *Ibid.*; the receipts totalled £325 9s. 6d.

[19] Bowyer, p. 217. For a detailed account of the play's late eighteenth- and nineteenth-century stage history, see Bowyer, pp. 217–218, on which my discussion is based.

[20] Norton, "Susanna Centlivre," p. 178.

One apparently insoluble problem exists regarding the play's authorship. Although in the Dedication Mrs. Centlivre claims complete originality, one of her fullest and most accurate contemporary biographers states that she had a collaborator: "In this Play she was assisted by Mr. Mottley, who wrote one or two entire Scenes of it."[21] The anonymous biographer is generally assumed to be John Mottley himself. Unfortunately, no known evidence exists by which to test his statement. The anonymous Prologue announces that the comedy is entirely Mrs. Centlivre's, including neither foreign nor native borrowings. More specifically, the writer states that "not one single tittle [is] from Molière." This protestation may be conventional, for eighteenth-century prologues and epilogues often disclaim debts to foreign plays, especially French ones, boasting questionable originality for English authors.[22] On the other hand, Mrs. Centlivre's dedicatory remarks cannot be disregarded, particularly since this is the only play for which she claims complete originality. That the comedy is stylistically and thematically consistent from beginning to end tends to support her statement. Presumably, she reworked any contributions that Mottley may have made.

Sources for specific episodes in the comedy have been suggested. Genest says that Mrs. Centlivre imitated Newburgh Hamilton's *Petticoat Plotter* in creating Simon Pure, the visiting Quaker whom Fainwell impersonates in order to outwit Prim.[23] Like the Colonel, Hamilton's True-love poses as a Quaker, Ananias Scribe, to gain entrance to Thrifty's house in order to court his daughter. As in *A Bold Stroke for a Wife*, when the real Scribe arrives, he is deemed an impostor and treated rudely. Unlike Prim, however, Thrifty himself discovers the fraud. Mrs. Centlivre's satire on Quakers may also be indebted to Cowley's *Guardian* (V.vi and xi), especially for the seduction of Tabitha and Mrs. Prim's rationalization of it (II.ii.30–44).[24] Reminiscent of *The Guardian* (V.i), too, is the Colonel's vision

[21] *A Compleat List of all the English Dramatic Poets, and of all Plays ever printed in the English Language to the present Year 1747*, appended to Thomas Whincop's *Scanderbeg: or, Love and Liberty* (London, 1747), p. 191.

[22] Mary E. Knapp, *Prologues and Epilogues of the Eighteenth Century* (New Haven, 1961), pp. 221–229, especially pp. 225–226; in discussing conventional protestations of originality, Miss Knapp refers to this Prologue, though she erroneously terms it the Epilogue.

[23] *Some Account of the English Stage* (Bath, 1832), II, 498–499.

[24] Professor James Sutherland has kindly called this possibility to my attention.

predicting his marriage to Mrs. Lovely, a ruse by which he accomplishes his aim (V.i.160–413). Yet, unlike Cowley's Cutter, Fainwell does not even try to dupe his beloved through this trick. To outwit her mother, Tabitha cooperates with Cutter by being well deceived; but Mrs. Lovely aids the Colonel directly in overcoming the Prims. Regarding the general satire on Quakers, Bowyer notes similarities between the Prims and Mrs. Plotwell, a character in Mrs. Centlivre's earlier comedy *The Beau's Duel* (1702).[25] Referring to this resemblance and that which Genest observes, he states that *A Bold Stroke for a Wife* often draws on earlier comedies. Several other parallels to Restoration plays are, in fact, evident.

Both uses of disguise in the gulling of Periwinkle (III.i and IV.iii) recall *Sir Martin Mar-all*. In Dryden's and Newcastle's play the landlord attempts to dispose of Sir Martin's rival by impersonating a mail carrier and informing Sir John that his father has died (II.ii). Disguised as a steward, Fainwell uses similar tactics against Periwinkle in their second encounter. But in contrast to Sir Martin Mar-all, he undertakes this stratagem himself, and his opponent is a guardian, not a suitor for Mrs. Lovely. When Sir Martin impersonates a traveler in trying to gull the Swashbuckler of his daughter (V.i), his antics more closely parallel the Colonel's first venture against Periwinkle. This episode in *A Bold Stroke for a Wife* also recalls the satire on the Royal Society in *The Virtuoso*. Although Shadwell employs no disguises that anticipate Mrs. Centlivre's, Sir Nicholas Gimcrack is a guardian; like Mrs. Lovely, the virtuoso's two wards lament their fate (I.ii). Still other similarities to earlier plays exist in *A Bold Stroke for a Wife*. Yet no one work can be termed a major source for this comedy. Even in the episodes just described, Mrs. Centlivre uses materials which had become the common property of contemporary writers: satires on Quakers and virtuosos abound in this period, as does delight in disguise.[26] That Mrs. Centlivre reshapes such conventional subjects with freshness surely justifies her protestation of originality.

A Bold Stroke for a Wife draws on contemporary literary traditions in

---

25 Bowyer, p. 215.

26 Regarding the period's preoccupation with disguise, especially in reference to comedy, see Norman N. Holland, chapter 6, "Disguise, Comic and Cosmic," *The First Modern Comedies: The Significance of Etherege, Wycherley and Congreve* (Cambridge, Mass., 1959). I discuss his thesis briefly below.

still other ways. All of the guardians and Mrs. Prim resemble character sketches of the period. A true descendant of Shadwell's Gimcrack, Periwinkle also recalls stereotyped characters of virtuosos in *The London Spy* (Pt. 1), *The Tatler* (No. 216), and *The Spectator* (Nos. 21 and 275). Tradelove's sharp practices and manic-depressive reactions to their success and failure find counterparts in Ward's *London Terrae-filius* (No. 5), his *London Spy* (Pt. 16), and Defoe's *Anatomy of Exchange-Alley* (1719). The changebroker's admiration for Dutch management is paralleled by contemporary characters whom Ward entitles "The English Foreigners; or, The Whigs turn'd Dutchmen."[27] With his pocket mirror and French inclinations, Sir Philip Modelove is an even more familiar type, one recurring throughout *The Tatler* and *The Spectator*; his dedication to ease and bachelorhood recalls the predilections of "Sir Narcissus Foplin: or, the Self-Admirer" in *Hickelty Pickelty: or A Medley Of Characters Adapted to the Age* (1708). Prim's hypocrisy, belief in inspired visions, and advocacy of the inner light are reminiscent of Quakerish speakers in a group of pamphlets initiated by *Aminadab, or the Quaker's Vision* (1710).[28] His wife's allusions to Biblical figures in arguing for home-spun feminine attire echo *The Scourge*, a contemporary periodical satirically characterizing Quakers.[29]

Although Mrs. Centlivre ridicules the guardians and Mrs. Prim, her primary aim is not didactic; unlike Shadwell, she does not even pretend to use humors characters to laugh men out of their follies. The guardians' eccentricities may be the butt of occasional satire; yet more often these characters serve merely to amuse, and Mrs. Centlivre's attack on them ends amiably. Despite their whimsicalities, we sense that everyone will live happily together after Fainwell succeeds in winning Mrs. Lovely. In any case, the guardians do not receive the lambasting essential to the Jonsonian tradition. Instead, their presence and function recall Sir William Temple's belief that the richness of English comedy derived from native humors types

---

[27] *The Poetical Entertainer* (1712), No. 3; see also No. 2.

[28] The pamphlets prompted by this one also appeared in 1710: *A Reply to Aminadab: or an Answer to the Quaker's Vision; Aminadab's Declaration delivered at a General Meeting holden upon the first day of the Pentecost;* and *Azarias, a Sermon held forth in a Quaker's Meeting immediately after Aminadab's Vision.*

[29] See No. 4, February 25, 1717.

who were to be tolerated.[30] Far from being benevolent, the four guardians cannot evoke the affectionate laughter accorded to eccentrics in later eighteenth-century literature. Still, they are not the targets for merciless ridicule that they would have been in most earlier comedy.

To differentiate between late seventeenth- and early eighteenth-century comedy can, of course, lead to artificial generalizations which obscure the continuity of a tradition. Probably no single tendency within it can be isolated as an exclusively early or late one. Temple's attitude regarding humors, for example, indicates the relatively early origins of tolerant laughter; and, as Norman N. Holland observes, even the first Restoration comedies contain strains of sentiment from which sentimentality could develop.[31] Nevertheless, as Clifford Leech demonstrates in a study of Congreve, changes in comic perspective and emphasis had begun to occur within the Restoration tradition by the end of the seventeenth century.[32] In the eighteenth century, comedy became more "homespun" and "less marked by the obvious contrivances of wit" than it had been in the Restoration.[33] *A Bold Stroke for a Wife* manifests these changes as well as others associated with the turn of the century.

Mrs. Centlivre's treatment of merchants in this comedy is more ambivalent than her use of humors characters.[34] Tradelove is ridiculed, as are merchants' wives and daughters (II.i.116, and II.ii.190); yet Freeman is heroic, and Tradelove's praise of mercantile contributions to English welfare is not intended ironically (II.ii.200–201, V.i.94–95, and V.i.99–105). With few exceptions, earlier comedies consistently ridicule merchants. But before Mrs. Centlivre wrote *A Bold Stroke for a Wife*, Collier, Steele, Blackmore, and other reformers had effectively criticized dramatists for such

---

[30] *Of Poetry* (1690). For a discussion of the changing attitudes towards humors types, see Stuart M. Tave, *The Amiable Humorist: A Study in the Comic Theory and Criticism of the Eighteenth and Early Nineteenth Centuries* (Chicago, 1960), especially chapters 4 and 5.

[31] Holland, pp. 85, 113, 160.

[32] "Congreve and the Century's End," *Philological Quarterly*, XLI (1962), 275–293.

[33] *Ibid.*, p. 284.

[34] Regarding changing attitudes towards the mercantile class in Restoration comedy, see John Loftis, *Comedy and Society from Congreve to Fielding* (Stanford, Calif., 1959), especially pp. 33–35.

derision.[35] In arousing laughter at the mercantile class, Mrs. Centlivre may recall Restoration attitudes; however, as a friend of Steele's, she also echoes his patriotic defense of merchants in *The Englishman* of 1713 (Nos. 3 and 4).

As a more significant result of the reform movement, her comedy is freer of profanity and sexual innuendo than are most earlier plays.[36] Dispensing with a love chase, the hero and heroine have decided upon matrimony before the action opens. Like their Restoration predecessors, Fainwell and Mrs. Lovely find love without money impractical, but unlike the gay couples of earlier comedy, they engage in no verbal sparring.[37] Bold as Fainwell may be, he is not a rake; nor is he referred to as a reformed rake. Saucy as Mrs. Lovely is, her prayer for his success (I.ii.66–70) is tinged with sentimentality. In their most pensive moods, a Millamant or Harriet would be reluctant to utter this plea or Mrs. Lovely's subsequent avowal to Fainwell, "Thou best of men, Heaven meant to bless me sure, when first I saw thee" (V.i.226–227).

The intrigue of the outwitting games which form the comedy's plot precludes frequent intrusions of such sentimentality. It also obscures the sentimentality of the situation which gives rise to the action. Like the heroines of popular romances, Mrs. Lovely is a damsel in distress whom a hero must rescue. This situation contrasts markedly with anti-heroic and harshly realistic attitudes about the sexes predominating in earlier Restoration comedy. Mrs. Lovely's plight is, in fact, reminiscent of fairy tales: her father hated posterity and therefore arranged to have his daughter permanently confined. Freeman terms this conduct "unnatural" (I.i.81), and Sackbut describes Lovely as "the most whimsical, out-of-the-way tempered man I ever heard of" (I.i.72–73). He was, apparently, even more eccentric than the guardians whom he appointed to govern his daughter. Just as their behavior causes more amusement than ridicule, so, too, do the events which originate in his last will and testament.

According to Dryden, a situation arising from such behavior is bound to create farce rather than comedy. In the Preface to *An Evening's Love; or the Mock Astrologer* (1671), he defines the difference

[35] See Loftis, pp. 30–35.

[36] Regarding these aspects of the reform movement, see Loftis, pp. 24–33.

[37] John Harrington Smith traces changing attitudes towards love and marriage in Restoration comedy: *The Gay Couple in Restoration Comedy* (Cambridge, Mass., 1948).

between these genres with reference to natural and unnatural behavior: "Comedy consists, though of low persons, yet of natural actions and characters; I mean such humours, adventures, and designs, as are to be found and met with in the world. Farce, on the other side, consists of forced humours, and unnatural events. Comedy presents us with the imperfections of human nature: Farce entertains us with what is monstrous and chimerical."[38] Restoration comic theory and practice are too intricate to permit simple differentiation between comedy and farce; nevertheless, Dryden's comments are provocative in respect to *A Bold Stroke for a Wife*. Although the play is by no means pure farce, it abounds in farcical situations generated by Lovely's unnatural will.

In III.i, for example, we laugh not at the gulling of Periwinkle but at Fainwell's forced inventions and the operations of a trapdoor. Throughout the play, we are amused by the unlikeliness of the Colonel's disguises, as they interact with the guardians' unnatural capers. We do not laugh at a realistic Restoration outwitting match between the sexes or between young lovers and their parents. Here we are amused by a preposterous contest of incongruities, created and perpetuated by eccentrics. Yet once we accept the initial fiction of the humorous father and guardians, all else follows logically. The play's success emanates from this artistic consistency and from the sense of realism that it establishes within a basically unrealistic situation. When, for example, Mrs. Lovely feigns a Quaker conversion (V.i), her antics are farcical; however, the plot justifies this pose and its comic mode and thus makes both credible. Since the Colonel must impersonate a Quaker to gain Prim's consent to marry her, she must cooperate with his efforts. Mrs. Lovely's world is, after all, based on unnatural behavior.

If *A Bold Stroke for a Wife* is tolerantly humorous and often farcical, it is also witty; however, Mrs. Centlivre's wit is seldom rhetorical or fanciful.[39] She infrequently achieves the brilliantly racy repartee of earlier Restoration comedy with its witty similitudes and balanced parallelisms.[40] Rather, hers is the kind of wit that Corbyn Morris was

[38] *Essays of John Dryden*, ed. W. P. Ker (Oxford, 1900), I, 135–136.

[39] For a discussion of the wit characteristic of early Restoration comedy, see Thomas H. Fujimura, *The Restoration Comedy of Wit* (Princeton, 1952), chapter 2.

[40] Dale Underwood analyzes the nature of comic language and its relationship to wit in Restoration comedy: chapter 6, "The Comic Language," *Etherege and the Seventeenth-Century Comedy of Manners* (New Haven, 1957); see especially pp. 106–110.

to describe later in the century as "gay allusion." [41] In her dialogue, sound judgment does not create "What oft was thought, but ne'er so well expressed." Instead, it seeks out topical allusions that comment implicitly and aptly on the situation at hand. For this reason, Mrs. Centlivre's abundant references to social and political events require glossing to an extent that Congreve's witty comparisons do not.

The full humor and wit of Fainwell's first contest with Periwinkle (III.i) can unfold only if we know that his allusions to science and his smattering of Greek comment on projects of the Royal Society. His reference to "a learned physiognomist in Grand Cairo" (III.i.208) and Periwinkle's acceptance of this authority mock the Society for occasionally recognizing such charlatans as experimental scientists.[42] In IV.i, Tradelove's miscalculating efforts to manipulate the stock market allude wittily to contemporary scandals in which overreached sharpers had to flee the town when they could not make good their wagers (see too IV.ii.102–116).[43] Sir Philip's and the Colonel's allusions to Heidegger's entertainments (II.i.109–111) suggest, without specifying, reports about the license associated with masquerades.[44] As these examples may imply, range of allusion, rather than development of particular references, characterizes Mrs. Centlivre's wit. If her facility of allusion is an intellectual limitation, nonetheless, it creates as much pleasure as does her evident ease in manipulating the play's plot.

Although witty repartee is not Mrs. Centlivre's forte, her use of language in this play is workmanlike and lively. So realistic is her scene at Jonathan's Coffee House (IV.i) that a mid-eighteenth-century commentator on the stock market commends the accuracy and vividness of her dialogue.[45] More significant is Mrs. Centlivre's use of expressive neologisms. The compound *simon-pure*, meaning

[41] *An Essay towards Fixing the True Standards of Wit, Humour, Raillery, Satire, and Ridicule* (London, 1744), p. 14.

[42] See R. F. Jones, "The Background of the Attack on Science in the Age of Pope," *Pope and his Contemporaries: Essays presented to George Sherburn*, ed. James L. Clifford and Louis A. Landa (Oxford, 1949), pp. 111–112.

[43] See John Francis, *Chronicles and Characters of the Stock Exchange* (London, 1849), pp. 58–65, especially pp. 61–62; see too [Daniel Defoe], *The Anatomy of Exchange-Alley: or, a System of Stock-Jobbing* (London, 1719), reprinted as an appendix by Francis, pp. 359–383.

[44] See *Freeholder*, No. 44, *Guardian*, No. 154, and an advertisement in *Spectator*, No. 22.

[45] [Thomas Mortimer], *Every Man his own Broker: or, a Guide to Exchange-Alley*, 2d ed. (London, 1761), p. 133.

genuine, entered the language through her creation of a character in this play.[46] Her use of *put* in reference to stockjobbing (IV.i.22) is the first recorded occurrence of this term cited by the *OED*. More interesting is her yet unacknowledged use of the substantive *poluflosboio* (III.i.141), a Greek loan meaning *loud roaring*. Under the adjectival form of this word (*polyphloisboian* or *poluphloisboian*) the *OED* enters a noun, *polyphloisboioism*, crediting *Blackwood's Magazine* (1823) with its first appearance in English; the adjective is said to occur first in 1824. That Mrs. Centlivre employs this esoteric borrowing with wit and accuracy again suggests her deftness in manipulating language.

Significant as they may be, neither this kind of linguistic skill nor topical wit can explain the continuing success of *A Bold Stroke for a Wife* over two centuries. By the nineteenth century or even earlier, many of its topical allusions had become meaningless to audiences and readers. And a play is seldom if ever read by the general public or staged for its philological interest. More specifically dramatic achievements account for this comedy's popularity. In part, it must be attributed to cleverly wrought stage business, plot intrigue, and amusing male roles. However, structural unity and concentrated action contribute at least as much to the comedy's dramatic success. As Bowyer notes, all the play's incidents center on the protagonist, Fainwell, and a single concern which he announces as the comedy opens: his intention to win Mrs. Lovely.[47] Like tightly developed variations on a theme, the action employs varied devices to convey a repeating motif, without monotony or extraneous complications. It presents a cycle of repetitive episodes and settings, modifying and embellishing them with new details.

Five times Fainwell attempts to overreach the guardians. Although each opponent presents a unique challenge, each challenge is directed to the same end: obtaining written consent for Fainwell to marry Mrs. Lovely. Determinedly individual as the guardians are, they are also unified, by their common ward and their fundamental eccentricity. Like a chameleon, the Colonel adapts himself to each man's foible, feigning friendship and kindred spirit toward the opponent at hand. In frequent tavern interludes, we preview all five disguises from a different perspective, as the real Fainwell and his real

[46] Glosses for words and linguistic information in this edition are based on the *Oxford English Dictionary*, unless otherwise noted.
[47] Bowyer, p. 212.

friend, Freeman, plan them. Freeman enters the action against the eccentrics in miniature outwitting games, gulling Periwinkle (III.i) and Tradelove (IV.i and iv) in acts of feigned friendship. His games bear on the main action, enabling the Colonel to complete his contests with these guardians. As the play draws to a close, the real world of tavern plots merges with that of deceptive appearances. To signal the merger, Freeman arrives at Prim's house with all the other guardians. In their presence, Fainwell assumes his true identity, after rapidly recapitulating all five contests.

To prevent monotony, Mrs. Centlivre varies the tempo of the outwitting games. The first, against Sir Philip, takes place in one uninterrupted episode, concluding successfully. The second, against Periwinkle, is also a single episode; however, it ends unsuccessfully, as chance intervenes and Periwinkle discovers the Colonel's real identity. Halfway through the play, this contest marks a turning point in Fainwell's fortunes, slowing down the action. Although the ensuing game against Tradelove is successful, it observes the retarded pace, going through three phases before reaching completion (IV.i, ii, and iv). As an added complication, it brings Freeman's outwitting match against Tradelove into action. Fainwell's third game is further complicated by being interwoven with the second against Periwinkle (IV.iii). Freeman initiates the latter before the third game commences, and the Colonel wins his second contest with Periwinkle while that with Tradelove is in progress. Through such contrapuntal treatment Mrs. Centlivre thickens the plot's texture, creating good-natured suspense.

Though a single episode, the Colonel's second match against Periwinkle introduces a significant variation on the basic pattern of outwitting games. In this venture, unlike any of the others, Fainwell disguises the marriage contract, presenting it as a lease in order to defeat his most troublesome opponent. Once he has brought Periwinkle to bay through this device, the action is again unimpeded; the match against Tradelove now moves rapidly to completion. As the action speeds forward, the gulling of the last guardian, Prim, takes place like that of the first, in one continuous episode which terminates successfully (V.i). As in the first game against Periwinkle, an outside party threatens to expose the Colonel's identity. But this time chance favors Fainwell, and he obtains the Quaker's signature before Simon Pure returns to disabuse Prim.

Despite their thematic repetitiveness, the outwitting contests create an impression of linear movement through space, as they take Fainwell to such varied settings as the Park and Exchange Alley. Nevertheless, two pivotal points exist to which the action always returns and on which it always turns, suggesting the motion of a cycle. They are the settings of the first act: the tavern, where Fainwell plots, and Prim's house, where Mrs. Lovely awaits him. Before Fainwell can claim his bride, he must successfully invade the Quaker's house. Twice he gains entry, and twice Mrs. Lovely almost upsets his plans because she fails to recognize him. Fainwell first arrives at Prim's after obtaining Sir Philip's consent (II.ii), and next when he returns as Simon Pure to gain the Quaker's. Although not identical, his two visits and Mrs. Lovely's responses to them reinforce the sense of repeating action observed in the gulling of Sir Philip and Prim. This impression is further strengthened because only in II.ii and V.i do all four guardians assemble. Three times they meet, always at Prim's house to discuss suitors for Mrs. Lovely. During Fainwell's first visit, their dissension quickly leads to his dismissal. Early in V.i, as if to blight his impending arrival, they reconvene to disagree, as in their first meeting. But by the end of Fainwell's second visit, when they last appear, he has resourcefully overcome their discord.

Fainwell's final triumph over the eccentrics marks the victory of concerted disguise. In V.i, Mrs. Lovely unwittingly dons her first deceptive costume and joins him in the game against Prim. Ironically, throughout the play she has scorned as hypocritical the Quaker garb that finally brings her liberation. Whenever we see her at Prim's house, she is as preoccupied by scorn for deceptive dress as Fainwell, in the tavern, is by plans for disguise. Before the guardians can be completely overreached, this difference in the hero's and heroine's attitudes must be reconciled. Like Fainwell, Mrs. Lovely must realize that disguise is not necessarily a mark of affectation or hyprocrisy. When she first appears on stage, she debates whether or not to put on the Quaker habit she detests (I.ii). After her next entrance (II.ii), she berates Mrs. Prim's hypocritical dress, having resolved not to wear it herself; by contrast, Fainwell now arrives, disguised as a beau, a breed he abhors as much as Mrs. Lovely does Quakers. Guided by necessity and realistic aims, he in no way shares Sir Philip's affectation. At the opening of the last act, just before his next arrival, Mrs. Lovely and Mrs. Prim echo their earlier conversation about clothing, but a significant change has occurred: for practical reasons, Mrs. Lovely has dressed as a Quaker. By altering her appearance, she hopes to silence Mrs. Prim's rebukes. During Fainwell's first visit, he has remarked, "How charming she appears" (II.ii.111–112). In his second visit to the Prims', he, too, echoes his earlier words, adding significantly to them: "How charming she appears, even in that disguise" (V.i.158–159). Once Mrs. Lovely discovers the full advantage of her dress, together she and Fainwell can play the final outwitting game to bring the action to a close.

Complication by disguise is a salient characteristic of Restoration comedy. It compliments the polite world's penchant for conducting intrigues and pranks in costumes and for attending masquerades. Accordingly, Holland interprets Wycherley's, Etherege's, and Congreve's use of this device as a mirror of court life.[48] He also believes disguise has more profound comic significance for these writers: it reflects the discrepancy between appearance and nature which the new science had disclosed.[49] In *A Bold Stroke for a Wife* disguise lacks this serious intellectual function. It simply fosters delight and a tightly developed plot. In a world of eccentrics where things are too much what they seem, only disguise can invert the orders of appearance and reality. And only disguise can place real people on an equal footing with humorous aberrations. That cleverly masked reality triumphs over unrealistic eccentricity is to be expected in the Augustan world to which this play belongs. In sentimental moments, Fainwell and Mrs. Lovely may feel that love conquers all things. But as intelligent people of fashion, they know that the god of love helps those who help themselves.

I am grateful to Professor James Sutherland for his guidance and to Professors Herbert Meritt, Michael Rewa, and Fred Robinson for help in translating Greek phrases. To my parents, whose patience has been endless, gratitude hardly seems a sufficient offering.

THALIA STATHAS

Indiana University

[48] Holland, pp. 47–50.
[49] Holland, pp. 54–58.

A BOLD STROKE FOR A WIFE

To His Grace Philip,
Duke and Marquis of Wharton, Etc.

My Lord,

   It has ever been the custom of poets to shelter productions
of this nature under the patronage of the brightest men
of their time; and 'tis observed that the Muses always met
the kindest reception from persons of the greatest merit.   5
The world will do me justice as to the choice of my patron
but will, I fear, blame my rash attempt in daring to address
your Grace and offer at a work too difficult for our ablest
pens, *viz.*, an encomium on your Grace. I have no plea
against such just reflections but the disadvantage of educa-   10
tion and the privilege of my sex.

   If your Grace discovers a genius so surprising in this
dawn of life, what must your riper years produce? Your
Grace has already been distinguished in a most peculiar
manner, being the first young nobleman that ever was   15
admitted into a House of Peers before he reached the age of
one and twenty. But your Grace's judgment and eloquence
soon convinced that august assembly that the excelling gifts
of nature ought not to be confined to time. We hope the
example which Ireland has set will shortly be followed by an   20
English House of Lords and your Grace made a member of
that body, to which you will be so conspicuous an ornament.

   Your good sense, and real love for your country, taught
your Grace to persevere in the principles of your glorious
ancestors by adhering to the defender of our religion and   25
laws; and the penetrating wisdom of your Royal Master saw
you merited your honors ere he conferred them. It is one of
the greatest glories of a monarch to distinguish where to
bestow his favors; and the world must do ours justice by
owning your Grace's titles most deservedly worn.   30

27. ere] *D2*; e'er *D1*.

0.1–2. *Philip . . . Etc.*] (1698–1731), second Marquis of Wharton, created
first Duke of Wharton in January, 1718; he had held and continued to hold
other titles, including a dukedom from the Pretender, whom he later
supported.
   16–17. *House . . . twenty*] Wharton had entered the Irish House of Lords
at nineteen.

It is with the greatest pleasure imaginable the friends of liberty see you pursuing the steps of your noble father. Your courteous, affable temper, free from pride and ostentation, makes your name adored in the country and enables your Grace to carry what point you please. The late Lord 35 Wharton will be still remembered by every lover of his country, which never felt a greater shock than what his death occasioned. Their grief had been inconsolable, if Heaven, out of its wonted beneficence to this favorite isle, had not transmitted all his shining qualities to you and, 40 phoenix-like, raised up one patriot out of the ashes of another.

That your Grace has a high esteem for learning particularly appears by the large progress you have made therein; and your love for the Muses shows a sweetness of temper and 45 generous humanity peculiar to the greatness of your soul; for such virtues reign not in the breast of every man of quality.

Defer no longer then, my Lord, to charm the world with the beauty of your numbers, and show the poet, as you have 50 done the orator. Convince our unthinking Britons by what vile arts France lost her liberty; and teach 'em to avoid their own misfortunes, as well as to weep over Henry IV, who (if it were possible for him to know) would forgive the bold assassin's hand for the honor of having his fall celebrated by 55 your Grace's pen.

To be distinguished by persons of your Grace's character is not only the highest ambition but the greatest reputation to an author; and it is not the least of my vanities to have it known to the public I had your Grace's leave to prefix 60 your name to this comedy.

I wish I were capable to clothe the following scenes in such a dress as might be worthy to appear before your Grace

---

32. *your noble father*] Thomas, first Marquis of Wharton (1648–1715), a Whig leader during the reigns of William III and Queen Anne.

51–53. *Convince . . . Henry IV*] Henry IV, King of France (1589–1610), had won tolerance for the Huguenots through religious wars; Louis XIV had ended this tolerance, as, Whigs believed, might the Pretender.

55. *assassin's hand*] Henry IV was assassinated by François Ravaillac, a religious fanatic who feared the king would besiege the pope.

and draw your attention, as much as your Grace's admirable qualifications do that of all mankind; but the Muses, like   65
most females, are least liberal to their own sex.

All I dare say in favor of this piece is that the plot is entirely new and the incidents wholly owing to my own invention, not borrowed from our own or translated from the works of any foreign poet; so that they have at least the   70
charm of novelty to recommend 'em. If they are so lucky in some leisure hour to give your Grace the least diversion, they will answer the utmost ambition of, my Lord,

> Your Grace's most obedient,
>   most devoted, and most humble servant,   75
>   Susanna Centlivre

76. Centlivre]   cent-livre D1–2.

PROLOGUE

By a Gentleman
Spoken by Mrs. Thurmond

Tonight we come upon a bold design,
To try to please without one borrowed line.
Our plot is new, and regularly clear,
And not one single tittle from Molière.
O'er buried poets we with caution tread,   5
And parish sextons leave to rob the dead.
For you, bright British fair, in hopes to charm ye,
We bring tonight a lover from the army.
You know the soldiers have the strangest arts,
Such a proportion of prevailing parts,   10
You'd think that they rid post to women's hearts.
I wonder whence they draw their bold pretense;
We do not choose them sure for our defense:
That plea is both impolitic and wrong,
And only suits such dames as want a tongue.   15
Is it their eloquence and fine address?
The softness of their language?—Nothing less.
Is it their courage, that they bravely dare
To storm the sex at once?—Egad, 'tis there.
They act by us as in the rough campaign,   20
Unmindful of repulses, charge again;
They mine and countermine, resolved to win,
And, if a breach is made—they will come in.
You'll think, by what we have of soldiers said,
Our female wit was in the service bred;   25
But she is to the hardy toil a stranger,
She loves the cloth, indeed, but hates the danger;
Yet to this circle of the brave and gay,
She bid me for her good intentions say,

PROLOGUE] *D1*; Rrologue *D2*.   4. Molière] Molleire *D1*; Moliere *D2*.

---

14. *That . . . wrong*] *impolitic* because the Tories pressed for eliminating the standing army in this peaceful period; the issue had reached its climax in January, 1718.

28. *circle . . . gay*] ladies in the center boxes.

She hopes you'll not reduce her to half pay.　　　　30
As for our play, 'tis English humor all;
Then will you let our manufacture fall?
Would you the honor of our nation raise,
Keep English credit up, and English plays.

---

30. *half pay*] reduced pay allowed to officers after the disbanding of their military units; this allowance had been substantially reduced in January, 1718; cf. I.i.64–65.

34. *Keep . . . up*] Support of public credit was a constant topic of concern and discussion. Public credit had improved in 1717.

DRAMATIS PERSONAE

Men

SIR PHILIP MODELOVE, an old beau		*Mr. Knap*
PERIWINKLE, a kind of a silly virtuoso	All Guardians to Mrs. Lovely	*Mr. Spiller*
TRADELOVE, a change-broker		*Mr. Bullock, Sr.* 5
OBADIAH PRIM, a Quaker [hosier]		*Mr. Pack*
COLONEL FAINWELL, in love with Mrs. Lovely		*Mr. Christopher Bullock* 10
FREEMAN, his friend, a merchant		*Mr. Ogden*
SIMON PURE, a Quaking preacher		*Mr. Griffin*
MR. SACKBUT, a tavern-keeper		*Mr. Hall* 15

Women

MRS. LOVELY, a fortune of thirty thousand pound	*Mrs. Bullock*
MRS. PRIM, wife to Prim the hosier	*Mrs. Kent*
BETTY, servant to Mrs. Lovely	*Mrs. Robins* 20

FOOTMEN, DRAWERS, ETC.

[Scene: *London*]

5. *Sr.*] sen. *D1–2*.   OBEBIAH *D2*.
7. OBADIAH] OBEDIAH *D1*;   9. *Christopher*] Chr. *D1*; Ch. *D2*.

---

3. *Periwinkle*] "one who surpasses or excels" (*OED*).
4. *virtuoso*] *obs.*, an experimental scientist and collector of specimens; often used disparagingly in reference to members of the Royal Society.
5–6. *changebroker*] exchange broker.

A Bold Stroke for a Wife

ACT I

[I.i]   *A tavern.*
Colonel Fainwell *and* Freeman *over a bottle.*

FREEMAN.

Come, Colonel, his Majesty's health! You are as melancholy
as if you were in love; I wish some of the beauties at Bath
ha'n't snapped your heart.

COLONEL.

Why faith, Freeman, there is something in't; I have seen a
lady at Bath who has kindled such a flame in me that all   5
the waters there can't quench.

FREEMAN.

Women, like some poisonous animals, carry their antidote
about 'em. Is she not to be had, Colonel?

COLONEL.

That's a difficult question to answer; however, I resolve
to try. Perhaps you may be able to serve me; you merchants   10
know one another. —The lady told me herself she was under
the charge of four persons.

FREEMAN.

Odso! 'Tis Mrs. Ann Lovely.

COLONEL.

The same; do you know her?

FREEMAN.

Know her! Ay—faith, Colonel, your condition is more   15

Title in D1 is followed by Etc.   *stage settings throughout both D1 and*
0.1. *A tavern*] SCENE *a Tavern*   *D2 but has been omitted in this edition.*
D1–2; "SCENE" *regularly precedes*

---

3. *snapped*] captured by surprise.
13. *Odso*] arch., a minced form of "Godso," an interjection used for
emphasis.

desperate than you imagine; why she is the talk and pity
of the whole town; and it is the opinion of the learned that
she must die a maid.

COLONEL.

Say you so? That's somewhat odd in this charitable city.
She's a woman, I hope.   20

FREEMAN.

For aught I know; but it had been as well for her had
nature made her any other part of the creation. The man
which keeps this house served her father; he is a very
honest fellow and may be of use to you; we'll send for him
to take a glass with us. He'll give you the whole history,   25
and 'tis worth your hearing.

COLONEL.

But may one trust him?

FREEMAN.

With your life; I have obligations enough upon him to
make him do anything; I serve him with wine.   *Knocks.*

COLONEL.

Nay, I know him pretty well myself; I once used to frequent   30
a club that was kept here.

Enter Drawer.

DRAWER.

Gentlemen, d'you call?

FREEMAN.

Ay, send up your master.

DRAWER.

Yes, sir.   *Exit.*

COLONEL.

Do you know any of this lady's guardians, Freeman?   35

FREEMAN.

Yes, I know two of them very well.

COLONEL.

What are they?

Enter Sackbut.

FREEMAN.

Here comes one will give you an account of them all—
Mr. Sackbut, we sent for you to take a glass with us.

'Tis a maxim among the friends of the bottle that as long   40
as the master is in company one may be sure of good wine.

SACKBUT.

Sir, you shall be sure to have as good wine as you send
in. —Colonel, your most humble servant; you are welcome
to town.

COLONEL.

I thank you, Mr. Sackbut.   45

SACKBUT.

I am as glad to see you as I should a hundred ton of
French claret custom free. My service to you, sir.   (*Drinks.*)
You don't look so merry as you used to do; are you not
well, Colonel?

FREEMAN.

He has got a woman in his head, landlord; can you help   50
him?

SACKBUT.

If 'tis in my power, I shan't scruple to serve my friend.

COLONEL.

'Tis one perquisite of your calling.

SACKBUT.

Ay, at t'other end of the town, where you officers use,
women are good forcers of trade; a well-customed house,   55
a handsome barkeeper, with clean, obliging drawers, soon
get the master an estate; but our citizens seldom do anything but cheat within the walls. —But as to the lady,
Colonel; point you at particulars, or have you a good
champagne stomach? Are you in full pay, or reduced,   60
Colonel?

COLONEL.

Reduced, reduced, landlord.

FREEMAN.

To the miserable condition of a lover!

62. landlord] *D2*; lanlord *D1*.

40–41. '*Tis . . . wine*] Adulteration of wine was a current problem.
47. *French . . . free*] High tariffs maintained on French wines to encourage
wine trade with other countries led to smuggling of claret into England.
54–58. *Ay . . . walls*] a reference to one of numerous contemporary
gambling houses, probably in the West End.

SACKBUT.

> Pish! That's preferable to half pay; a woman's resolution
> may break before the peace; push her home, Colonel;   65
> there's no parlying with that sex.

COLONEL.

> Were the lady her own mistress I have some reasons to
> believe I should soon command in chief.

FREEMAN.

> You know Mrs. Lovely, Mr. Sackbut?

SACKBUT.

> Know her! Ay, poor Nancy; I have carried her to school   70
> many a frosty morning. Alas, if she's the woman, I pity
> you, Colonel. Her father, my old master, was the most
> whimsical, out-of-the-way tempered man I ever heard of,
> as you will guess by his last will and testament. This
> was his only child. I have heard him wish her dead a   75
> thousand times.

COLONEL.

> Why so?

SACKBUT.

> He hated posterity, you must know, and wished the world
> were to expire with himself. He used to swear if she had
> been a boy, he would have qualified him for the opera.   80

FREEMAN.

> 'Tis a very unnatural resolution in a father.

SACKBUT.

> He died worth thirty thousand pounds, which he left to
> this daughter provided she married with the consent of
> her guardians. But that she might be sure never to do so,
> he left her in the care of four men, as opposite to each   85
> other as light and darkness. Each has his quarterly rule,
> and three months in a year she is obliged to be subject
> to each of their humors, and they are pretty different, I
> assure you. She is just come from Bath.

84. guardians] *D2*; guaadians *D1*.

---

70. *Nancy*] often interchanged with "Ann," probably through confusion
of a diminutive form of *ME Annis*, "Agnes," with "Ann."

80. *qualified . . . opera*] castrated him; a reference to Italian *castrati*
singing in opera.

COLONEL.

'Twas there I saw her.   90

SACKBUT.

Ay, sir, the last quarter was her beau guardian's. She
appears in all public places during his reign.

COLONEL.

She visited a lady who boarded in the same house with me.
I liked her person and found an opportunity to tell her
so. She replied she had no objection to mine, but if I   95
could not reconcile contradictions, I must not think of
her, for that she was condemned to the caprice of four
persons who never yet agreed in any one thing, and she was
obliged to please them all.

SACKBUT.

'Tis most true, sir; I'll give you a short description of   100
the men and leave you to judge of the poor lady's condition.
One is a kind of a virtuoso, a silly, half-witted fellow
but positive and surly; fond of nothing but what is antique
and foreign, and wears his clothes of the fashion of the
last century; dotes upon travelers and believes Sir John   105
Mandeville more than the Bible.

COLONEL.

That must be a rare old fellow!

SACKBUT.

Another is a changebroker, a fellow that will outlie the
devil for the advantage of stock and cheat his father that
got him in a bargain. He is a great stickler for trade and   110
hates everything that wears a sword.

FREEMAN.

He is a great admirer of the Dutch management and swears
they understand trade better than any nation under the sun.

SACKBUT.

The third is an old beau that has May in his fancy and
dress but December in his face and his heels; he admires   115

---

105. *travelers*] The Royal Society were interested in and published
travelers' accounts of their adventures.

105–106. *Sir John Mandeville*] the supposed author of a fanciful medieval
travel account, popular in the early eighteenth century (see *Tatler*, No. 254).

112–113. *Dutch . . . sun*] The Dutch were known for shrewdness in trade
and finance.

nothing but new fashions, and those must be French; loves operas, balls, masquerades, and is always the most tawdry of the whole company on a birthday.

COLONEL.

These are pretty opposite to one another, truly. And the fourth, what is he, landlord?   120

SACKBUT.

A very rigid Quaker, whose quarter begun this day. I saw Mrs. Lovely go in not above two hours ago. Sir Philip set her down. What think you now, Colonel; is not the poor lady to be pitied?

COLONEL.

Ay, and rescued too, landlord.   125

FREEMAN.

In my opinion, that's impossible.

COLONEL.

There is nothing impossible to a lover. What would not a man attempt for a fine woman and thirty thousand pounds? Besides, my honor is at stake; I promised to deliver her, and she bade me win her and take her.   130

SACKBUT.

That's fair, faith.

FREEMAN.

If it depended upon knight-errantry, I should not doubt your setting free the damsel; but to have avarice, impertinence, hypocrisy, and pride at once to deal with requires more cunning than generally attends a man of honor.   135

COLONEL.

My fancy tells me I shall come off with glory; I resolve to try, however. —Do you know all the guardians, Mr. Sackbut?

SACKBUT.

Very well, sir; they all use my house.

COLONEL.

And will you assist me, if occasion be?   140

SACKBUT.

In everything I can, Colonel.

FREEMAN.

I'll answer for him; and whatever I can serve you in, you

---

117. *tawdry*] showy.

may depend on. I know Mr. Periwinkle and Mr. Tradelove;
the latter has a very great opinion of my interest abroad.
I happened to have a letter from a correspondent two hours   145
before the news arrived of the French king's death; I
communicated it to him; upon which he bought up all the
stock he could, and what with that and some wagers
he laid, he told me he had got to the tune of five hundred
pounds; so that I am much in his good graces.   150

COLONEL.

I don't know but you may be of service to me, Freeman.

FREEMAN.

If I can, command me, Colonel.

COLONEL.

Is it not possible to find a suit of clothes ready-made at
some of these sale shops, fit to rig out a beau, think you,
Mr. Sackbut?   155

SACKBUT.

O hang 'em, no, Colonel; they keep nothing ready-made
that a gentleman would be seen in. But I can fit you with
a suit of clothes, if you'd make a figure—velvet and gold
brocade—they were pawned to me by a French count
who had been stripped at play and wanted money to carry   160
him home; he promised to send for them, but I have heard
nothing from him.

FREEMAN.

He has not fed upon frogs long enough yet to recover his
loss, ha, ha.

COLONEL.

Ha, ha; well, those clothes will do, Mr. Sackbut, though   165
we must have three or four fellows in tawdry liveries.
Those can be procured, I hope.

FREEMAN.

Egad, I have a brother come from the West Indies that can
match you; and, for expedition sake, you shall have his

---

146. *French king's death*] Louis XIV had died in September, 1715.

154. *sale shops*] dealers in cheap clothing, especially in Monmouth Street,
St. Giles.

163–164. *fed . . . loss*] Frogs' legs, a delicacy in France, were ridiculed in
England as cheap fare (cf. Steele's *The Tender Husband*, V.ii).

169. *match you*] supply you suitably.

servants. There's a black, a tawny-moor, and a Frenchman. 170
They don't speak one word of English, so can make no
mistake.

COLONEL.

Excellent. Egad, I shall look like an Indian prince. First
I'll attack my beau guardian. Where lives he?

SACKBUT.

Faith, somewhere about St. James's; though to say in what 175
street, I cannot. But any chairman will tell you where
Sir Philip Modelove lives.

FREEMAN.

O, you'll find him in the Park at eleven every day; at
least I never passed through at that hour without seeing
him there. But what do you intend?   180

COLONEL.

To address him in his own way and find what he designs
to do with the lady.

FREEMAN.

And what then?

COLONEL.

Nay, that I can't tell, but I shall take my measures
accordingly.   185

SACKBUT.

Well, 'tis a mad undertaking, in my mind; but here's to
your success, Colonel.   *Drinks.*

COLONEL.

'Tis something out of the way, I confess; but fortune may
chance to smile, and I succeed. Come, landlord, let me
see those clothes.—Freeman, I shall expect you'll leave word 190
with Mr. Sackbut where one may find you upon occasion;
and send my equipage of India immediately, do you hear?

FREEMAN.

Immediately.   *Exit.*

---

170. *tawny-moor*] tawny-skinned foreigner; probably first applied to
Africans.

175. *St. James's*] St. James's Palace and Park in the West End.

176. *chairman*] one who carried people in a chairlike vehicle.

178. *the Park*] St. James's Park, known as "the Park," where noon was
the fashionable hour in good weather.

192. *equipage*] retinue of liveried servants.

COLONEL.

>Bold was the man who ventured first to sea,
>But the first vent'ring lovers bolder were.   195
>The path of love's a dark and dangerous way,
>Without a landmark, or one friendly star,
>And he that runs the risk, deserves the fair.

Exit [*with* Sackbut].

[I.ii]   *Prim's house.*
Enter Mrs. Lovely *and her maid* Betty.

BETTY.

Bless me, madam! Why do you fret and tease yourself so?
This is giving them the advantage with a witness.

MRS. LOVELY.

Must I be condemned all my life to the preposterous humors
of other people; and pointed at by every boy in town?—
O! I could tear my flesh, and curse the hour I was born.   5
Is it not monstrously ridiculous that they should desire to
impose their Quaking dress upon me at these years? When
I was a child, no matter what they made me wear; but now—

BETTY.

I would resolve against it, madam; I'd see 'em hanged
before I'd put on the pinched cap again.   10

MRS. LOVELY.

Then I must never expect one moment's ease; she has rung
such a peal in my ears already that I shan't have the right
use of them this month—what can I do?

BETTY.

What can you not do, if you will but give your mind to it?
Marry, madam.   15

MRS. LOVELY.

What! And have my fortune go to build churches and
hospitals?

BETTY.

Why, let it go. If the Colonel loves you, as he pretends,
he'll marry you without a fortune, madam; and I assure you,

12. shan't] *D2*; shant *D1*.

10. *pinched cap*] the usual headdress of Quakeresses; steeple-shaped, with
ample coverage for modesty.

a Colonel's lady is no despicable thing; a Colonel's post   20
will maintain you like a gentlewoman, madam.

MRS. LOVELY.

So you would advise me to give up my own fortune and
throw myself upon the Colonel's.

BETTY.

I would advise you to make yourself easy, madam.

MRS. LOVELY.

That's not the way, I am sure. No, no, girl, there are   25
certain ingredients to be mingled with matrimony, without
which I may as well change for the worse as for the better.
When the woman has fortune enough to make the man
happy, if he has either honor or good manners, he'll make
her easy. Love makes but a slovenly figure in that house   30
where poverty keeps the door.

BETTY.

And so you resolve to die a maid, do you, madam?

MRS. LOVELY.

Or have it in my power to make the man I love master of my
fortune.

BETTY.

Then you don't like the Colonel so well as I thought you   35
did, madam, or you would not take such a resolution.

MRS. LOVELY.

It is because I do like him, Betty, that I take such a
resolution.

BETTY.

Why, do you expect, madam, the Colonel can work
miracles? Is it possible for him to marry you with the consent   40
of all your guardians?

MRS. LOVELY.

Or he must not marry me at all, and so I told him; and he
did not seem displeased with the news. He promised to
set me free, and I, on that condition, promised to make
him master of that freedom.   45

BETTY.

Well, I have read of enchanted castles, ladies delivered

44. that condition] *D1*; the condition *D2*.

from the chains of magic, giants killed, and monsters overcome; so that I shall be the less surprised if the Colonel
should conjure you out of the power of your guardians. If he
does, I am sure he deserves your fortune.   50

MRS. LOVELY.

And shall have it, girl, if it were ten times as much; for I'll
ingenuously confess to thee that I do like the Colonel
above all men I ever saw. There's something so *jantée* in a
soldier, a kind of a *je ne sais quoi* air that makes 'em more
agreeable than the rest of mankind. They command   55
regard, as who should say, "We are your defenders; we
preserve your beauties from the insults of rude unpolished
foes and ought to be preferred before those lazy indolent
mortals who, by dropping into their father's estate, set
up their coaches and think to rattle themselves into our   60
affections."

BETTY.

Nay, madam, I confess that the army has engrossed all
the prettiest fellows. A laced coat and feather have irresist-
ible charms.

MRS. LOVELY.

But the Colonel has all the beauties of the mind, as well   65
as person. —O all ye powers that favor happy lovers,
grant he may be mine! Thou god of love, if thou be'st
aught but name, assist my Fainwell.

      Point all thy darts to aid my love's design,
      And make his plots as prevalent as thine.   70

---

49. conjure you] *D1*; conjure your
D2.
70.] *D1 and D2 append* "The End of

the First ACT." *Similar phrases appearing at the conclusions of all Acts in D1
and D2 have been omitted in this edition.*

---

53. *jantée*] Although Mrs. Centlivre treats this as a French word, the
OED enters it as an early form of "jaunty," accented on the second syllable:
dashing.
54. *je . . . quoi*] This phrase had gained currency in seventeenth-century
aesthetics to describe the indefinable effect of grace or charm on the senses.

ACT II

[II.i]   *The Park.*
          Enter Colonel, *finely dressed, three Footmen after him.*

COLONEL.

    So, now if I can but meet this beau—egad, methinks I
cut a smart figure and have as much of the tawdry air as
any Italian count or French marquis of 'em all. Sure I
shall know this knight again—ha, yonder he sits, making
love to a mask, i'faith. I'll walk up the Mall and come   5
down by him.   *Exit.*

Scene draws and discovers Sir Philip *upon a bench with a* Woman, *masked.*

SIR PHILIP.

    Well, but, my dear, are you really constant to your keeper?

WOMAN.

    Yes, really sir. —Hey day, who comes yonder? He cuts a
mighty figure.

SIR PHILIP.

    Ha! A stranger by his equipage keeping so close at his   10
heels—he has the appearance of a man of quality—
positively French by his dancing air.

WOMAN.

    He crosses as if he meant to sit down here.

SIR PHILIP.

    He has a mind to make love to thee, child.

      Enter Colonel *and seats himself upon the bench by* Sir Philip.

WOMAN.

    It will be to no purpose if he does.   15

SIR PHILIP.

    Are you resolved to be cruel then?

COLONEL.

    You must be very cruel, indeed, if you can deny anything
to so fine a gentleman, madam.   *Takes out his watch.*

3. marquis] marquée *D1–2.*   4. ha] *D1*; ah *D2.*

---

    5. *a mask*] a masked woman; although silk and velvet masks were
fashionable, they were often associated with prostitutes.
    5. *Mall*] a fashionable promenade adjoining the Park.
    14. *child*] a form of contemptuous or affectionate address.

WOMAN.

I never mind the outside of a man.

COLONEL.

And I'm afraid thou art no judge of the inside.   20

SIR PHILIP.

I am positively of your mind, sir, for creatures of her function
seldom penetrate beyond the pocket.

WOMAN (*aside*).

Creatures of your composition have, indeed, generally more
in their pockets than in their heads.

SIR PHILIP (*pulling out his watch*).

Pray, what says your watch? Mine is down.   25

COLONEL.

I want thirty-six minutes of twelve, sir.

Puts up his watch and takes out his snuffbox.

SIR PHILIP.

May I presume, sir?

COLONEL.

Sir, you honor me.   *Presenting the box.*

SIR PHILIP [*aside*].

He speaks good English, though he must be a foreigner.—
[*Aloud.*] This snuff is extremely good and the box pro-   30
digious fine; the work is French, I presume, sir.

COLONEL.

I bought it in Paris, sir; I do think the workmanship
pretty neat.

SIR PHILIP.

Neat, 'tis exquisitely fine, sir. Pray, sir, if I may take
the liberty of inquiring, what country is so happy to claim   35
the birth of the finest gentleman in the universe? France, I
presume.

COLONEL.

Then you don't think me an Englishman?

SIR PHILIP.

No, upon my soul don't I.

COLONEL.

I am sorry for't.   40

26. thirty-six] 36 *D1–2.*

SIR PHILIP.

Impossible you should wish to be an Englishman! Pardon me, sir, this island could not produce a person of such alertness.

COLONEL.

As this mirror shows you, sir—

Puts up a pocket glass to Sir Philip's *face.*

WOMAN [*aside*].

Coxcombs; I'm sick to hear 'em praise one another. One   45
seldom gets anything by such animals, not even a dinner,
unless one can dine upon soup and celery.   *Exit.*

SIR PHILIP.

O Ged, sir!— [*Calls after her.*]   Will you leave us, madam?
Ha, ha.

COLONEL.

She fears 'twill be only losing time to stay here, ha, ha.—I   50
know not how to distinguish you, sir, but your mien and
address speak you *Right Honorable.*

SIR PHILIP.

Thus great souls judge of others by themselves. I am only
adorned with knighthood, that's all, I assure you, sir; my
name is Sir Philip Modelove.   55

COLONEL.

Of French extraction?

SIR PHILIP.

My father was French.

COLONEL.

One may plainly perceive it. There is a certain gaiety
peculiar to my nation (for I will own myself a Frenchman),
which distinguishes us everywhere. A person of your figure   60
would be a vast addition to a coronet.

SIR PHILIP.

I must own I had the offer of a barony about five years
ago, but I abhorred the fatigue which must have attended
it. I could never yet bring myself to join with either party.

45. Coxcombs] *D2*; Coxcomb's *D1*.   47. celery] sallery *D1–2*.

---

47. *soup and celery*] a reference to fashionable but unsubstantial French
delicacies.

48. *Ged*] *rare* or *arch.*, variant of "Gad," a minced pronunciation of "God,"
used in oaths.

COLONEL.

You are perfectly in the right, Sir Philip; a fine person   65
should not embark himself in the slovenly concern of
politics. Dress and pleasure are objects proper for the soul of
a fine gentleman.

SIR PHILIP.

And love—

COLONEL.

O, that's included under the article of pleasure.   70

SIR PHILIP.

Parbleu, il est un homme d'esprit; I must embrace you.   (*Rises
and embraces.*)   Your sentiments are so agreeable to mine
that we appear to have but one soul, for our ideas and
conceptions are the same.

COLONEL (*aside*).

I should be sorry for that.— [*Aloud.*]   You do me too   75
much honor, Sir Philip.

SIR PHILIP.

Your vivacity and *jantée* mien assured me at first sight
there was nothing of this foggy island in your composition.
May I crave your name, sir?

COLONEL.

My name is La Fainwell, sir, at your service.   80

SIR PHILIP.

The La Fainwells are French, I know; though the name is
become very numerous in Great Britain of late years. I was
sure you was French the moment I laid my eyes upon you;
I could not come into the supposition of your being an
Englishman. This island produces few such ornaments.   85

COLONEL.

Pardon me, Sir Philip, this island has two things superior to
all nations under the sun.

SIR PHILIP.

Ay? What are they?

COLONEL.

The ladies and the laws.

77. and] *D2*; and and *D1*.   84. into] in to *D1–2*.

---

77. *jantée*] *obs.*, "jaunty," genteel; cf. I.ii.53.

SIR PHILIP.

The laws indeed do claim a preference of other nations,   90
but by my soul, there are fine women everywhere. I must
own I have felt their power in all countries.

COLONEL.

There are some finished beauties, I confess, in France,
Italy, Germany, nay, even in Holland; *mais sont bien rares.*
But *les belles Anglaises!* O, Sir Philip, where find we   95
such women? Such symmetry of shape! Such elegancy of
dress! Such regularity of features! Such sweetness of
temper! Such commanding eyes! And such bewitching
smiles?

SIR PHILIP.

Ah! *Parbleu, vous êtes attraper.*   100

COLONEL.

Non, je vous assure, chevalier, but I declare there is no amusement so agreeable to my *goût* as the conversation of a fine
woman. I could never be prevailed upon to enter into what
the vulgar calls the pleasure of the bottle.

SIR PHILIP.

My own taste, *positivement.* A ball or a masquerade is 105
certainly preferable to all the productions of the vine-
yard.

COLONEL.

Infinitely. I hope the people of quality in England will
support that branch of pleasure which was imported with
their peace and since naturalized by the ingenious Mr. 110
Heidegger.

SIR PHILIP.

The ladies assure me it will become part of the constitution,
upon which I subscribed an hundred guineas; it will be of

94. *rares*] *rare D1–2.*   113. an hundred] *D1*; a hundred
                                 D2.

109–110. *branch . . . peace*] masquerades, which the French ambassador,
the Duke d'Aumont, had popularized in London after the Peace of Utrecht
(1713).

111. *Heidegger*] John James Heidegger (1659?–1749), a Swiss presenting
masquerades at the Haymarket. He was known as the *"surintendant des
plaisirs d'Angleterre."*

great service to the public, at least to the company of
surgeons and the City in general.   115

COLONEL.

Ha, ha, it may help to ennoble the blood of the City. Are
you married, Sir Philip?

SIR PHILIP.

No, nor do I believe I ever shall enter into that honorable
state; I have an absolute tender for the whole sex.

COLONEL (aside).

That's more than they have for you, I dare swear.   120

SIR PHILIP.

And I have the honor to be very well with the ladies, I can
assure you, sir, and I wòn't affront a million of fine women
to make one happy.

COLONEL.

Nay, marriage is really reducing a man's taste to a kind
of half pleasure, but then it carries the blessing of peace 125
along with it; one goes to sleep without fear and wakes
without pain.

SIR PHILIP.

There is something of that in't; a wife is a very good dish
for an English stomach—but gross feeding for nicer palates,
ha, ha, ha.   130

COLONEL.

I find I was very much mistaken. I imagined you had been
married to that young lady which I saw in the chariot
with you this morning in Gracechurch Street.

SIR PHILIP.

Who, Nancy Lovely? I am a piece of a guardian to that
lady, you must know; her father, I thank him, joined me 135

128. There is] *D1*; There's *D2*.

114–115. *service . . . surgeons*] a reference to fees for treating venereal
disease or performing abortions.
115. *City*] the financial district of London, associated with citizens and
commerce rather than the gentry and the nobility.
116. *ennoble . . . City*] Citizens' wives and daughters were often derisively
accused of being promiscuous with the nobility; cf. II.ii.190.
119. *tender*] obs., tender feeling.
133. *Gracechurch Street*] a street in the City, intersecting Lombard and
Fenchurch Streets, where Quaker shopkeepers congregated.

with three of the most preposterous old fellows, that, upon my soul, I'm in pain for the poor girl. She must certainly lead apes, as the saying is. Ha, ha.

COLONEL.

That's pity, Sir Philip; if the lady would give me leave, I would endeavor to avert that curse. 140

SIR PHILIP.

As to the lady, she'd gladly be rid of us at any rate, I believe; but here's the mischief: he who marries Miss Lovely must have the consent of us all four, or not a penny of her portion. For my part, I shall never approve of any but a man of figure, and the rest are not only averse to 145 cleanliness but have each a peculiar taste to gratify. For my part, I declare, I would prefer you to all men I ever saw.

COLONEL.

And I her to all women.

SIR PHILIP.

I assure you, Mr. Fainwell, I am for marrying her, for 150 I hate the trouble of a guardian, especially among such wretches, but resolve never to agree to the choice of any one of them, and I fancy they'll be even with me, for they never came into any proposal of mine yet.

COLONEL.

I wish I had your leave to try them, Sir Philip. 155

SIR PHILIP.

With all my soul, sir, I can refuse a person of your appearance nothing.

COLONEL.

Sir, I am infinitely obliged to you.

SIR PHILIP.

But do you really like matrimony?

COLONEL.

I believe I could with that lady, sir. 160

SIR PHILIP.

The only point in which we differ; but you are master of so many qualifications that I can excuse one fault, for I

---

138. *lead . . . is*] Old maids were said to lead apes in hell as a penalty for having remained single.

must think it a fault in a fine gentleman, and that you are
such, I'll give it under my hand.

COLONEL.

I wish you'd give me your consent to marry Mrs. Lovely 165
under your hand, Sir Philip.

SIR PHILIP.

I'll do't, if you'll step into St. James's Coffee House,
where we may have pen and ink; though I can't foresee
what advantage my consent will be to you without you
could find a way to get the rest of the guardians', but I'll 170
introduce you; however, she is now at a Quaker's where
I carried her this morning, when you saw us in Gracechurch Street. I assure you she has an odd *ragoût* of guardians, as you will find when you hear the characters,
which I'll endeavor to give you as we go along.— [*Calls* 175
the Servants.] Hey, Pierre, Jacques, Renno, where are
you all, scoundrels? Order the chariot to St. James's
Coffee House.

COLONEL.

Le noir, le brun, le blanc—mortbleu, où sont ces coquins-là?
Allons, monsieur le chevalier.   180

SIR PHILIP.

Ah, *pardonnez-moi, monsieur.*   [*Offers to follow him.*]

COLONEL [*refusing to go first*].

Not one step, upon my soul, Sir Philip.

SIR PHILIP.

The best bred man in Europe, positively.   *Exeunt.*

[II.ii]   *Obadiah Prim's house.*
                Enter Mrs. Lovely, *followed by* Mrs. Prim.

MRS. PRIM.

Then thou wilt not obey me; and thou dost really think
those fallals becometh thee?

---

179. *le brun*] *article in D1 is in-*   0.1.] *D1 and D2 read* "SCENE
distinct (le *or* la); *la brun D2.*   *changes to*" *before the stage setting here*
[II.ii]   *and at the opening of IV.iii and IV.iv.*

---

173. *ragoût*] *fig.*, a peppery mixture; the *OED* enters this French loan,
citing Mrs. Centlivre's usage here in exemplifying it.
[II.ii]
2. *fallals*] a reduplicating formation connoting gaudiness.

MRS. LOVELY.

I do, indeed.

MRS. PRIM.

Now will I be judged by all sober people, if I don't look
more like a modest woman than thou dost, Ann.   5

MRS. LOVELY.

More like a hypocrite, you mean, Mrs. Prim.

MRS. PRIM.

Ah, Ann, Ann, that wicked Philip Modelove will undo thee.
Satan so fills thy heart with pride during the three months of
his guardianship that thou becomest a stumbling block
to the upright.   10

MRS. LOVELY.

Pray, who are they? Are the pinched cap and formal hood
the emblems of sanctity? Does your virtue consist in your
dress, Mrs. Prim?

MRS. PRIM.

It doth not consist in cut hair, spotted face, and bare
necks. O, the wickedness of this generation! The primi-   15
tive women knew not the abomination of hooped petti-
coats.

MRS. LOVELY.

No, nor the abomination of cant neither. Don't tell me,
Mrs. Prim, don't. I know you have as much pride, vanity,
self-conceit, and ambition among you, couched under that   20
formal habit and sanctified countenance, as the proudest
of us all; but the world begins to see your prudery.

MRS. PRIM.

Prudery! What, do they invent new words as well as new
fashions? Ah, poor fantastic age, I pity thee—poor deluded
Ann. Which dost thou think most resemblest the saint   25
and which the sinner, thy dress or mine? Thy naked
bosom allureth the eye of the bystander, encourageth
the frailty of human nature, and corrupteth the soul with
evil longings.

MRS. LOVELY.

And pray, who corrupted your son Tobias with evil long-   30

23–24. *Prudery . . . fashions*] *prudery*: prudishness; a recent borrowing
from French first known to occur in *Tatler*, No. 126.

ings? Your maid Tabitha wore a handkerchief, and yet he
made the saint a sinner.

MRS. PRIM.

Well, well, spit thy malice. I confess Satan did buffet
my son Tobias and my servant Tabitha; the evil spirit was
at that time too strong, and they both became subject to 35
its workings, not from any outward provocation but from
an inward call. He was not tainted with the rottenness of
the fashions, nor did his eyes take in the drunkenness
of beauty.

MRS. LOVELY.

No! That's plainly to be seen. 40

MRS. PRIM.

Tabitha is one of the faithful; he fell not with a stranger.

MRS. LOVELY.

So! Then you hold wenching no crime, provided it be
within the pale of your own tribe? You are an excellent
casuist, truly.

Enter Obadiah Prim.

PRIM.

Not stripped of thy vanity yet, Ann! —Why dost not 45
thou make her put it off, Sarah?

MRS. PRIM.

She will not do it.

PRIM.

Verily, thy naked breasts troubleth my outward man;
I pray thee hide 'em, Ann. Put on a handkerchief, Ann
Lovely. 50

MRS. LOVELY.

I hate handkerchiefs when 'tis not cold weather, Mr. Prim.

MRS. PRIM.

I have seen thee wear a handkerchief—nay, and a mask to
boot—in the middle of July.

MRS. LOVELY.

Ay, to keep the sun from scorching me.

PRIM.

If thou couldst not bear the sunbeams, how dost thou think 55
man should bear thy beams? Those breasts inflame desire;
let them be hid, I say.

MRS. LOVELY.

Let me be quiet, I say. Must I be tormented thus forever?
Sure no woman's condition ever equaled mine; foppery, folly,
avarice, and hypocrisy are by turns my constant companions,   60
and I must vary shapes as often as a player. I cannot
think my father meant this tyranny. No, you usurp an
authority which he never intended you should take.

PRIM.

Hark thee, dost thou call good counsel tyranny? Do I or
my wife tyrannize when we desire thee in all love to put off   65
thy tempting attire and veil thy provokers to sin?

MRS. LOVELY.

Deliver me, good Heaven! Or I shall go distracted.

Walks about.

MRS. PRIM.

So! Now thy pinners are tossed and thy breasts pulled up.
Verily, they were seen enough before; fie upon the filthy
tailor who made them stays.   70

MRS. LOVELY.

I wish I were in my grave! Kill me rather than treat me
thus.

PRIM.

Kill thee! Ha, ha, thou think'st thou are acting some
lewd play, sure—kill thee! Art thou prepared for death,
Ann Lovely? No, no, thou wouldst rather have a husband,   75
Ann. Thou wantest a gilt coach with six lazy fellows behind
to flant it in the Ring of vanity, among the princes and
rulers of the land who pamper themselves with the fat-
ness thereof. But I will take care that none shall squander
away thy father's estate; thou shalt marry none such,   80
Ann.

MRS. LOVELY.

Would you marry me to one of your own canting sex?

---

68. *pinners*] a fashionable cap with long side flaps.
74. *lewd*] *obs.*, bad, worthless.
77. *flant it*] *obs.*, quasi-transitive form of "flaunt."
77. *Ring of vanity*] an oval track at the entrance to Hyde Park, around
which people of fashion rode in their coaches.

PRIM.

Yea, verily, none else shall ever get my consent, I do
assure thee, Ann.

MRS. LOVELY.

And I do assure thee, Obadiah, that I will as soon turn   85
papist and die in a convent.

MRS. PRIM.

O wickedness!

MRS. LOVELY.

O stupidity!

PRIM.

O blindness of heart!

MRS. LOVELY [*aside to* Prim].

Thou blinder of the world, don't provoke me, lest I betray   90
your sanctity and leave your wife to judge of your purity.
What were the emotions of your spirit when you squeezed
Mary by the hand last night in the pantry, when she
told you you bussed so filthily? Ah, you had no aversion
to naked bosoms when you begged her to show you a little,   95
little, little bit of her delicious bubby. Don't you remember
those words, Mr. Prim?

MRS. PRIM.

What does she say, Obadiah?

PRIM.

She talketh unintelligibly, Sarah.— (*Aside.*)   Which way
did she hear this? This should not have reached the ears 100
of the wicked ones; verily, it troubleth me.

Enter Servant.

SERVANT.

Philip Modelove, whom they call Sir Philip, is below and
such another with him; shall I send them up?

PRIM.

Yea.   *Exit* [Servant].

83. none . . . my consent] *D1*; no   94. filthily] *D2*; fiithily *D1*.
ne . . . my onsent *D2*.   104. S.D. *Exit* [Servant] *Exit*
90. lest] *D2*; least *D1*.   *appears after l. 103 in D1 and D2.*

Enter Sir Philip *and* Colonel.

SIR PHILIP.

How dost thou do, Friend Prim?— [*To* Mrs. Prim.]　Odso, 105
my she-friend here too! What, you are documenting Miss
Nancy, reading her a lecture upon the pinched coif, I
warrant ye.

MRS. PRIM.

I am sure thou never readest her any lecture that was good.
— [*Aside.*]　My flesh riseth so at these wicked ones that pru- 110
dence adviseth me to withdraw from their sight.　　　*Exit.*

COLONEL (*aside*).

O, that I could find means to speak to her. How charming
she appears. I wish I could get this letter into her hand.

SIR PHILIP.

Well, Miss Cocky, I hope thou has got the better of them.

MRS. LOVELY.

The difficulties of my life are not to be surmounted, Sir 115
Philip.— (*Aside.*)　I hate the impertinence of him as much
as the stupidity of the other.

PRIM.

Verily, Philip, thou wilt spoil this maiden.

SIR PHILIP.

I find we still differ in opinion; but that we may none of
us spoil her, prithee, Prim, let us consent to marry her. 120
I have sent for our brother guardians to meet me here
about that very thing. —Madam, will you give me leave to
recommend a husband to you? Here's a gentleman which,
in my mind, you can have no objection to.

　　　　　　　　Presents the Colonel *to her; she looks another way.*

MRS. LOVELY (*aside*).

Heaven deliver me from the formal and the fantastic fool. 125

COLONEL.

A fine woman, a fine horse, and fine equipage are the
finest things in the universe. And if I am so happy to
possess you, madam, I shall become the envy of mankind,
as much as you outshine your whole sex.

---

114. *Cocky*] diminutive form of "cock," male fowl, once used as a term of
endearment.

As he takes her hand to kiss it, he endeavors to put the letter into it; she lets it drop; Prim takes it up.

MRS. LOVELY.

I have no ambition to appear conspicuously ridiculous, 130
sir.   *Turning from him.*

COLONEL.

So falls the hopes of Fainwell.

MRS. LOVELY (*aside*).

Ha! Fainwell! 'Tis he. What have I done? Prim has the
letter, and all will be discovered.

PRIM.

Friend, I know not thy name, so cannot call thee by it; but 135
thou seest thy letter is unwelcome to the maiden; she will
not read it.

MRS. LOVELY.

Nor shall you. (*Snatches the letter.*) I'll tear it in a
thousand pieces and scatter it, as I will the hopes of all
those that any of you shall recommend to me.   140
                                                 Tears the letter.

SIR PHILIP.

Ha! Right woman, faith.

COLONEL (*aside*).

Excellent woman.

PRIM.

Friend, thy garb savoreth too much of the vanity of the
age for my approbation; nothing that resembleth Philip
Modelove shall I love, mark that. Therefore, Friend 145
Philip, bring no more of thy own apes under my roof.

SIR PHILIP.

I am so entirely a stranger to the monsters of thy breed
that I shall bring none of them, I am sure.

COLONEL (*aside*).

I am likely to have a pretty task by that time I have gone
through them all; but she's a city worth taking, and egad, 150
I'll carry on the siege. If I can but blow up the outworks, I
fancy I am pretty secure of the town.

132. falls] *D1*; fall *D2*.

Enter Servant.

SERVANT (*to* Sir Philip).

Toby Periwinkle and Thomas Tradelove demandeth to see
thee.

SIR PHILIP.

Bid them come up.   [*Exit* Servant.] 155

MRS. LOVELY [*aside*].

Deliver me from such an inundation of noise and nonsense.
O, Fainwell! Whatever thy contrivance is, prosper it
Heaven—but O, I fear thou never canst redeem me.   *Exit.*

SIR PHILIP.

Sic transit gloria mundi!

Enter Mr. Periwinkle *and* Tradelove.

(*Aside to the* Colonel.)   These are my brother guardians, 160
Mr. Fainwell; prithee observe the creatures.

TRADELOVE.

Well, Sir Philip, I obey your summons.

PERIWINKLE.

Pray, what have you to offer for the good of Mrs. Lovely,
Sir Philip?

SIR PHILIP.

First, I desire to know what you intend to do with that 165
lady. Must she be sent to the Indies for a venture, or live to
be an old maid and then entered amongst your curiosities
and shown for a monster, Mr. Periwinkle?

COLONEL (*aside*).

Humph, curiosities. That must be the virtuoso.

PERIWINKLE.

Why, what would you do with her?   170

SIR PHILIP.

I would recommend this gentleman to her for a husband, sir,
a person whom I have picked out from the whole race of
mankind.

---

159. *Sic . . . mundi*] "Thus passes away the glory of the world," a phrase
associated with Christian asceticism.

167. *curiosities*] cabinets of specimens assembled by virtuosos for
study.

PRIM.

I would advise thee to shuffle him again with the rest of
mankind, for I like him not.   175

COLONEL.

Pray, sir, without offense to your formality, what may be
your objections?

PRIM.

Thy person; thy manners; thy dress; thy acquaintance—thy
everything, friend.

SIR PHILIP.

You are most particularly obliging, friend, ha, ha.   180

TRADELOVE.

What business do you follow, pray sir?

COLONEL (aside).

Humph, by that question he must be the broker.— [Aloud.]
Business, sir! The business of a gentleman.

TRADELOVE.

That is as much as to say you dress fine, feed high, lie with
every woman you like, and pay your surgeon's bills better 185
than your tailor's or your butcher's.

COLONEL.

The court is much obliged to you, sir, for your character of a
gentleman.

TRADELOVE.

The court, sir! What would the court do without us citizens?

SIR PHILIP.

Without your wives and daughters, you mean, Mr. Trade- 190
love?

PERIWINKLE.

Have you ever traveled, sir?

COLONEL [aside].

That question must not be answered now.— [Aloud.]   In
books I have, sir.

PERIWINKLE.

In books? That's fine traveling indeed! —Sir Philip, 195
when you present a person I like, he shall have my consent
to marry Mrs. Lovely; till when, your servant.   Exit.

---

185. pay ... bills] payment for treating venereal disease.

COLONEL (*aside*).

> I'll make you like me before I have done with you, or I am
> mistaken.

TRADELOVE.

> And when you can convince me that a beau is more useful 200
> to my country than a merchant, you shall have mine; till
> then, you must excuse me.   *Exit.*

COLONEL (*aside*).

> So much for trade. I'll fit you too.

SIR PHILIP.

> In my opinion, this is very inhumane treatment as to the
> lady, Mr. Prim.   205

PRIM.

> Thy opinion and mine happens to differ as much as our
> occupations, friend. Business requireth my presence and
> folly thine, and so I must bid thee farewell.   *Exit.*

SIR PHILIP.

> Here's breeding for you, Mr. Fainwell. Gad take me, I'd
> give half my estate to see these rascals bit.   210

COLONEL (*aside*).

> I hope to bite you all, if my plots hit.

---

203. *fit you*] ?*obs.*, when object is a person: to provide with what is
necessary.

210. *bit*] *colloquial*, gulled and gloated over; now only used in the passive,
but see l. 211.

ACT III

The tavern.

Sackbut *and the* Colonel *in an Egyptian dress.*

SACKBUT.

A lucky beginning, Colonel. You have got the old beau's consent.

COLONEL.

Ay, he's a reasonable creature; but the other three will require some pains. Shall I pass upon him, think you? Egad, in my mind I look as antique as if I had been pre- 5 served in the ark.

SACKBUT.

Pass upon him! Ay, ay, as roundly as white wine dashed with sack does for mountain and sherry, if you have but assurance enough.

COLONEL.

I have no apprehension from that quarter; assurance is the 10 cockade of a soldier.

SACKBUT.

Ay, but the assurance of a soldier differs much from that of a traveler. Can you lie with a good grace?

COLONEL.

As heartily, when my mistress is the prize, as I would meet the foe when my country called and king commanded; so 15 don't you fear that part; if he don't know me again, I'm safe. I hope he'll come.

SACKBUT.

I wish all my debts would come as sure. I told him you had been a great traveler, had many valuable curiosities, and was a person of a most singular taste; he seemed trans- 20 ported and begged me to keep you till he came.

COLONEL.

Ay, ay, he need not fear my running away. Let's have a bottle of sack, landlord; our ancestors drank sack.

7–8. *white . . . sherry*] a reference to misrepresenting certain blends of white wines for more expensive ones. *Sack:* a class of Spanish or Canary white wines; *mountain:* white wine made from mountain-grown Malaga grapes.

SACKBUT.

> You shall have it.

COLONEL.

> And whereabouts is the trap door you mentioned? · · · 25

SACKBUT.

> There's the conveyance, sir. · · · *Exit.*

COLONEL.

> Now, if I should cheat all these roguish guardians and carry
> off my mistress in triumph, it would be what the French
> call a *grand coup d'éclat*—odso! Here comes Periwinkle.
> Ah, deuce take this beard; pray Jupiter it does not give · · 30
> me the slip and spoil all.

> > *Enter* Sackbut *with wine, and* Periwinkle *following.*

SACKBUT.

> Sir, this gentleman, hearing you have been a great traveler
> and a person of fine speculation, begs leave to take a glass
> with you; he is a man of a curious taste himself.

COLONEL.

> The gentleman has it in his face and garb. —Sir, you are · · 35
> welcome.

PERIWINKLE.

> Sir, I honor a traveler and men of your inquiring dis-
> position. The oddness of your habit pleases me extremely;
> 'tis very antique, and for that I like it.

COLONEL.

> It is very antique, sir. This habit once belonged to the · · 40
> famous Claudius Ptolemeus, who lived in the year a
> hundred and thirty-five.

SACKBUT *(aside).*

> If he keeps up to the sample, he shall lie with the devil
> for a bean-stack, and win it every straw.

PERIWINKLE.

> A hundred and thirty-five! Why, that's prodigious now— · · 45

40. It is] *D1*; 'Tis *D2*.

---

41. *Claudius Ptolemeus*] the famous Alexandrian mathematician, astron-
omer, and geographer of the second century A.D.

43–44. *lie . . . straw*] In Scottish witchcraft, the *bean-stack* functioned like a
broomstick but was made from beanstalks, or beanstraw. *Lie* may be a pun,
since witches won their powers by copulating with the devil.

well, certainly 'tis the finest thing in the world to be a
traveler.

COLONEL.

For my part, I value none of the modern fashions of a fig
leaf.

PERIWINKLE.

No more do I, sir; I had rather be the jest of a fool than   50
his favorite. I am laughed at here for my singularity. This
coat, you must know, sir, was formerly worn by that
ingenious and very learned person John Tradescant.

COLONEL.

John Tradescant! Let me embrace you, sir. John Tradescant was my uncle, by mother side; and I thank you for   55
the honor you do his memory; he was a very curious man
indeed.

PERIWINKLE.

Your uncle, sir! Nay then, 'tis no wonder that your taste
is so refined; why, you have it in your blood—my humble
service to you, sir. To the immortal memory of John   60
Tradescant, your never-to-be-forgotten uncle.   *Drinks.*

COLONEL.

Give me a glass, landlord.

PERIWINKLE.

I find you are primitive even in your wine. Canary was
the drink of our wise forefathers; 'tis balsamic and
saves the charge of apothecaries' cordials. —O, that   65
I had lived in your uncle's days! Or rather, that he
were now alive. O, how proud he'd be of such a nephew.

SACKBUT (*aside*).

O pox! That would have spoiled the jest.

---

53. *John Tradescant*] (1608–1662), an antiquarian, traveler, and gardener,
whose curiosities founded the Ashmolean Museum at Oxford.

54–55. *John . . . uncle*] Tradescant left no descendants; the Colonel's
pose and muff (l. 120) may allude to a well-known contemporary pseudo-
virtuoso, James Salter, a barber claiming descent from Tradescant; his
muff was famous.

60–61. *To . . . uncle*] In 1717, Elias Ashmole's diary had been published
posthumously; since he nowhere adequately credits Tradescant's contribu-
tion to his fame, Mrs. Centlivre may be deliberately doing so here.

PERIWINKLE.

A person of your curiosity must have collected many
rarities.   70

COLONEL.

I have some, sir, which are not yet come ashore, as an
Egyptian's idol.

PERIWINKLE.

Pray, what might that be?

COLONEL.

It is, sir, a kind of an ape which they formerly worshipped
in that country. I took it from the breast of a female   75
mummy.

PERIWINKLE.

Ha, ha, our women retain part of their idolatry to this
day, for many an ape lies on a lady's breast, ha, ha.

SACKBUT (*aside*).

A smart old thief.

COLONEL.

Two tusks of an hippopotamus, two pair of Chinese nut-   80
crackers, and one Egyptian mummy.

PERIWINKLE.

Pray, sir, have you never a crocodile?

COLONEL.

Humph, the boatswain brought one with design to show it,
but touching at Rotterdam and hearing it was no rarity in
England, he sold it to a Dutch poet.   85

SACKBUT.

The devil's in that nation; it rivals us in everything.

72. Egyptian's idol] Egyptians idol   80. hippopotamus] hippotamus
D1; Egyptian idol *D2*.   *D1–2*.

---

78. *ape*] *obs.*, fool. This may refer to Pope, whose name was often abbrevi-
ated "A. P-pe" (see Bowyer, p. 205); his farce *Three Hours After Marriage*
(1717) is undoubtedly intended in the reference to the mummy and the
crocodile (ll. 81 ff.). Because of his deformity, Pope was often termed an ape
by critics of the farce's lewd monsters.

84–85. *hearing . . . it*] During a stage accident in the fourth performance
of *Three Hours After Marriage*, the crocodile indulged in amorous highjinks,
hastening the demise of the farce. The monster's costume was reassigned to
an afterpiece, *The Shipwreck: or, Perseus and Andromeda*.

85. *Dutch poet*] probably Colley Cibber, "the Hollander," who had
revived the scandal of the mummy and the crocodile earlier in 1718,
while performing *The Rehearsal*.

PERIWINKLE.

I should have been very glad to have seen a living crocodile.

COLONEL.

My genius led me to things more worthy my regard. Sir,
I have seen the utmost limits of this globular world; I   90
have seen the sun rise and set; know in what degree of heat
he is at noon to the breadth of a hair, and what quantity
of combustibles he burns in a day, how much of it turns
to ashes and how much to cinders.

PERIWINKLE.

To cinders? You amaze me, sir; I never heard that the   95
sun consumed anything. Descartes tells us—

COLONEL.

Descartes, with the rest of his brethren, both ancient
and modern, knew nothing of the matter. I tell you,
sir, that nature admits an annual decay, though im-
perceptible to vulgar eyes. Sometimes his rays destroy 100
below, sometimes above. You have heard of blazing comets,
I suppose?

PERIWINKLE.

Yes, yes, I remember to have seen one; and our astrologers
tell us of another which shall happen very quickly.

COLONEL.

Those comets are little islands bordering on the sun, 105

96. Descartes] *D2*; Discartes *D1*.   97. Descartes] *D2*; Diseartes *D1*.

91–92. *know . . . hair*] Whiston, Halley, Keill, and other scientists had
studied the sun's position and heat at given latitudes, hours, and seasons.

95–96. *cinders . . . us*] In *Le Monde*, Descartes speculated about sun
spots; he also discussed the relation of flames to cinders. Although he did not
relate cinders to sun spots, Derham and Fontenelle termed the spots smoky
particles emitted by the sun.

97–98. *ancient and modern*] a reference to contemporary debate attempting
to determine who were superior, the ancients or the moderns.

99. *nature . . . decay*] Those favoring the ancients over the moderns
argued that nature was in a state of progressive decay.

101. *comets*] Newton, Halley, Flamsteed, and Whiston had increased
knowledge about and interest in comets.

103. *I . . . one*] perhaps the famous comet of 1680 which had been visible
for four months.

103–104. *astrologers . . . quickly*] Halley had plotted the orbits and cycles
of comets recorded since 1337; he predicted that the comet of 1682 would
return in 1758.

which at certain times are set on fire by that luminous
body's moving over them perpendicular, which will one
day occasion a general conflagration.

SACKBUT (*aside*).

One need not scruple the Colonel's capacity, faith.

PERIWINKLE.

This is marvelous strange. These cinders are what I never 110
read of in any of our learned dissertations.

COLONEL (*aside*).

I don't know how the devil you should.

SACKBUT (*aside*).

He has it at his fingers' ends; one would swear he had
learned to lie at school, he does it so cleverly.

PERIWINKLE.

Well, you travelers see strange things. Pray, sir, have you 115
any of those cinders?

COLONEL.

I have, among my other curiosities.

PERIWINKLE.

O, what have I lost for want of traveling! Pray, what
have you else?

COLONEL.

Several things worth your attention. I have a muff made 120
of the feathers of those geese that saved the Roman Capitol.

PERIWINKLE.

Is't possible?

SACKBUT (*aside*).

Yes, if you are such a goose to believe him.

COLONEL.

I have an Indian leaf which, open, will cover an acre of

113. it at his] *D1*; at this *D2*.

---

108. *general conflagration*] Those arguing for nature's decay foresaw a
general fire which would purge or even destroy the earth. In *The New Theory
of the Earth*, Whiston stated that the comet of 1680 had caused the Great
Deluge and would return to cause a "General Conflagration."

121. *geese . . . Capitol*] When the Gauls tried to seize the Capitol by night,
the sacred geese supposedly cackled, waking guards.

land, yet folds up into so little a compass you may put it 125
into your snuffbox.

SACKBUT (*aside*).

Humph! That's a thunderer.

PERIWINKLE.

Amazing!

COLONEL.

Ah, mine is but a little one; I have seen some of them
that would cover one of the Caribbean Islands.   130

PERIWINKLE.

Well, if I don't travel before I die, I shan't rest in my grave.
Pray, what do the Indians with them?

COLONEL.

Sir, they use them in their wars for tents, the old women
for riding hoods, the young for fans and umbrellas.

SACKBUT (*aside*).

He has a fruitful invention.   135

PERIWINKLE.

I admire our East India Company imports none of them;
they would certainly find their account in them.

COLONEL (*aside*).

Right, if they could find the leaves.— [*Aloud.*]   Look ye,
sir, do you see this little vial?

PERIWINKLE.

Pray you, what is it?   140

COLONEL.

This is called *poluflosboio*.

PERIWINKLE.

Poluflosboio! It has a rumbling sound.

COLONEL.

Right, sir, it proceeds from a rumbling nature. This water
was part of those waves which bore Cleopatra's vessel
when she sailed to meet Anthony.   145

125. into so] *D1*; in so *D2*.

---

136. *East India Company*] an English joint stock company, trading in
India.
141–142. *poluflosboio . . . sound*] a Greek echoic word, "loud roaring"; a
humorous Homeric epithet for the sea.

PERIWINKLE.

Well, of all that ever traveled, none had a taste like you.

COLONEL.

But here's the wonder of the world: this, sir, is called *zona*, or *moros musphonon*; the virtues of this is inestimable.

PERIWINKLE.

Moros musphonon! What in the name of wisdom can that be? To me it seems a plain belt.   150

COLONEL.

This girdle has carried me all the world over.

PERIWINKLE.

You have carried it, you mean.

COLONEL.

I mean as I say, sir. Whenever I am girded with this, I am invisible; and, by turning this little screw, can be in the court of the Great Mogul, the Grand Signior, and 155 King George in as little time as your cook can poach an egg.

PERIWINKLE.

You must pardon me, sir; I can't believe it.

COLONEL.

If my landlord pleases, he shall try the experiment immediately.   160

SACKBUT.

I thank you kindly, sir, but I have no inclination to ride post to the devil.

COLONEL.

No, no, you shan't stir a foot; I'll only make you-invisible.

SACKBUT.

But if you could not make me visible again—   165

---

147. *zona*] Latin form of Greek *zone*, girdle, or an attempt to reproduce the sound of the Greek word itself, ending–[e].

148. *moros musphonon*] *moros*: Greek, "foolish"; *musphonon*: esoteric Greek, "mousebane," an aconite herb. Perhaps a circumlocution, disregarding Greek inflections: "mousetrap for a fool" or "foolish mousetrap"; in cant "mousetrap" meant "a ruse to destroy or defeat someone."

155–156. *Great . . . George*] respectively, the courts of the Mahommedan emperor of Delhi, the Turkish potentate of Constantinople, and George I of England.

PERIWINKLE.

Come, try it upon me, sir; I am not afraid of the devil,
nor all his tricks. 'Sbud, I'll stand 'em all.

COLONEL.

There, sir, put it on. —Come, landlord, you and I must face
the east. (*They turn about*). —Is it on, sir?

PERIWINKLE.

'Tis on.   *They turn about again.* 170

SACKBUT.

Heaven protect me! Where is he?

PERIWINKLE.

Why here, just where I was.

SACKBUT.

Where, where, in the name of virtue? Ah, poor Mr.
Periwinkle! —Egad, look to't, you had best, sir, and
let him be seen again, or I shall have you burnt for a 175
wizard.

COLONEL.

Have patience, good landlord.

PERIWINKLE.

But really, don't you see me now?

SACKBUT.

No more than I see my grandmother that died forty years
ago.   180

PERIWINKLE.

Are you sure you don't lie? Methinks I stand just where
I did, and see you as plain as I did before.

SACKBUT.

Ah, I wish I could see you once again!

COLONEL.

Take off the girdle, sir.   *He takes it off.*

SACKBUT.

Ah, sir, I am glad to see you with all my heart. 185
                                       Embraces him.

PERIWINKLE.

This is very odd; certainly there must be some trick in't—
pray, sir, will you do me the favor to put it on yourself?

---

167. *'Sbud*], *obs.*, euphemistic form of "'Sblood": "by His blood," or
"God's blood," or short for "God's bodikins."

COLONEL.

With all my heart.

PERIWINKLE.

But first I'll secure the door.

COLONEL.

You know how to turn the screw, Mr. Sackbut.   190

SACKBUT.

Yes, yes—come, Mr. Periwinkle, we must turn full east.

They turn; the Colonel *sinks down a trap door.*

COLONEL.

'Tis done; now turn.   *They turn.*

PERIWINKLE.

Ha! Mercy upon me! My flesh creeps upon my bones—this must be a conjurer, Mr. Sackbut.

SACKBUT.

He is the devil, I think.   195

PERIWINKLE.

O! Mr. Sackbut, why do you name the devil, when perhaps he may be at your elbow.

SACKBUT.

At my elbow! Marry, Heaven forbid.

COLONEL (*below*).

Are you satisfied, sir?

PERIWINKLE.

Yes, sir, yes—how hollow his voice sounds!   200

SACKBUT.

Yours seemed just the same. Faith, I wish this girdle were mine; I'd sell wine no more. Hark ye, Mr. Periwinkle (*takes him aside till the* Colonel *rises again*), if he would sell this girdle, you might travel with great expedition.

COLONEL.

But it is not to be parted with for money.   205

PERIWINKLE.

I am sorry for't, sir, because I think it the greatest curiosity I ever heard of.

COLONEL.

By the advice of a learned physiognomist in Grand Cairo, who consulted the lines in my face, I returned to England, where, he told me, I should find a rarity in the keeping 210 of four men, which I was born to possess for the benefit of

mankind, and the first of the four that gave me his consent,
I should present him with this girdle. Till I have found
this jewel, I shall not part with the girdle.

PERIWINKLE.

What can that rarity be? Did he not name it to you?   215

COLONEL.

Yes, sir; he called it a chaste, beautiful, unaffected
woman.

PERIWINKLE.

Pish! Women are no rarities. I never had any great taste
that way. I married, indeed, to please a father, and I
got a girl to please my wife; but she and the child (thank 220
Heaven) died together. Women are the very gewgaws of the
creation, playthings for boys which, when they write man,
they ought to throw aside.

SACKBUT (*aside*).

A fine lecture to be read to a circle of ladies.

PERIWINKLE.

What woman is there, dressed in all the pride and foppery 225
of the times, can boast of such a foretop as the cockatoo?

COLONEL (*aside*).

I must humor him.— [*Aloud.*] Such a skin as the
lizard?

PERIWINKLE.

Such a shining breast as the hummingbird?

COLONEL.

Such a shape as the antelope?   230

PERIWINKLE.

Or, in all the artful mixture of their various dresses, have
they half the beauty of one box of butterflies?

COLONEL.

No, that must be allowed—for my part, if it were not
for the benefit of mankind, I'd have nothing to do with
them, for they are as indifferent to me as a sparrow or a 235
flesh fly.

226. cockatoo] cockatoor *D1–2*.

---

226. *cockatoo*] a member of the parrot family, known for its brilliant
crest.

235. *sparrow*] probably ironic, since sparrows have traditionally been
associated with lechery.

236. *flesh fly*] *fig.*, a predatory and lecherous person.

PERIWINKLE.

Pray, sir, what benefit is the world to reap from this
lady?

COLONEL.

Why, sir, she is to bear me a son, who shall restore the art
of embalming and the old Roman manner of burying their   240
dead; and, for the benefit of posterity, he is to discover the
longitude, so long sought for in vain.

PERIWINKLE.

Od! These are very valuable things, Mr. Sackbut.

SACKBUT (*aside*).

He hits it off admirably and t'other swallows it like sack
and sugar.— [*To* Periwinkle.]   Certainly this lady must   245
be your ward, Mr. Periwinkle, by her being under the care
of four persons.

PERIWINKLE.

By the description it should.— (*Aside.*)   Egad, if I could
get that girdle, I'd ride with the sun, and make the tour of
the whole world in four and twenty hours.— [*To the* Colonel.]   250
And are you to give that girdle to the first of the four
guardians that shall give his consent to marry that lady,
say you, sir?

COLONEL.

I am so ordered, when I can find him.

PERIWINKLE.

I fancy I know the very woman. Her name is Ann Lovely.   255

COLONEL.

Excellent! He said, indeed, that the first letter of her name
was *L*.

PERIWINKLE.

Did he really? Well, that's prodigiously amazing, that a
person in Grand Cairo should know anything of my ward.

---

249. the tour] *D2*; th'tour *D1*.

240–241. *embalming . . . dead*] The Royal Society tried to discover the
secrets of both of these ancient burial methods.

242. *longitude*] Projects for discovering the longitude at sea had been
popular and unsuccessful since the reign of Charles II. Bishop Sprat had
said that its discovery would benefit "posterity."

243. *Od*] *arch.*, euphemism for "God."

COLONEL.

Your ward?   260

PERIWINKLE.

To be plain with you, sir, I am one of those four guardians.

COLONEL.

Are you indeed, sir? I am transported to find the man who
is to possess this *moros musphonon* is a person of so curious a
taste. Here is a writing drawn up by that famous Egyptian,
which, if you will please to sign, you must turn your face 265
full north, and the girdle is yours.

PERIWINKLE.

If I live till this boy is born, I'll be embalmed and sent
to the Royal Society when I die.

COLONEL.

That you shall most certainly.

Enter Drawer.

DRAWER.

Here's Mr. Staytape, the tailor, inquires for you, Colonel.   270

SACKBUT.

Who do you speak to, you son of a whore?

PERIWINKLE (*aside*).

Ha! Colonel!

COLONEL (*aside*).

Confound the blundering dog.

DRAWER.

Why, to Colonel—

SACKBUT.

Get you out, you rascal.   *Kicks him out, and exit after him.* 275

DRAWER [*leaving*].

What the devil is the matter?

COLONEL (*aside*).

This dog has ruined all my scheme, I see by Periwinkle's
looks.

263. possess] *D2*; profess *D1*.

270. *Staytape*] *cant*, tailor; from "staytape," a staylace used in tailoring.

PERIWINKLE.

How finely I should have been choused. Colonel, you'll
pardon me that I did not give you your title before; it 280
was pure ignorance, faith it was. Pray—hem, hem—
pray, Colonel, what post had this learned Egyptian in your
regiment?

COLONEL (aside).

A pox of your sneer.— [Aloud.]   I don't understand you,
sir.   285

PERIWINKLE.

No? That's strange. I understand you, Colonel—an
Egyptian of Grand Cairo! Ha, ha, ha. I am sorry such a well-
invented tale should do you no more service. We old fellows
can see as far into a millstone as him that picks it. I am not
to be tricked out of my trust; mark that.   290

COLONEL (aside).

The devil! I must carry it off; I wish I were fairly out.—
[Aloud.]   Look ye, sir, you may make what jest you please,
but the stars will be obeyed, sir, and, depend upon it,
I shall have the lady, and you none of the girdle.— (Aside.)
Now for Freeman's part of the plot.   295

                              Exit [unseen by Periwinkle].

PERIWINKLE.

The stars! Ha, ha, no star has favored you, it seems.
The girdle! Ha, ha, ha, none of your legerdemain tricks
can pass upon me. Why, what a pack of trumpery has this
rogue picked up. His *pagod*, *poluflosboios*, his *zonas*, *moros*
musphonons, and the devil knows what. But I'll take care—ha, 300
gone? Ay, 'twas time to sneak off.— [Calls out.]   Soho,
the house!

                         Enter Sackbut.

Where is this trickster? Send for a constable; I'll have

297. legerdemain] *D1* (*italicized and*   299. pagod] *D2*; *paegod D1*.
capitalized); *Lagerdemain's D2*.

___

279. *choused*] *colloquial,* tricked or cheated.
289. *see . . . it*] "Seeing into a millstone" is a proverbial protestation of
acuteness, often used ironically; a "mill-picker" shapes the grinding
surfaces of millstones.
299. *pagod*] an image of an Eastern deity.
301. *Soho*] a call to draw attention; from hunting.

this rascal before the Lord Mayor. I'll Grand Cairo him, with a pox to him. I believe you had a hand in putting 305 this imposture upon me, Sackbut.

SACKBUT.

Who, I, Mr. Periwinkle? I scorn it; I perceived he was a cheat and left the room on purpose to send for a constable to apprehend him, and endeavored to stop him when he went out; but the rogue made but one step from the stairs to 310 the door, called a coach, leapt into it, and drove away like the devil, as Mr. Freeman can witness, who is at the bar and desires to speak with you. He is this minute come to town.

PERIWINKLE.

Send him in. *Exit* Sackbut. 315

What a scheme this rogue had laid. How I should have been laughed at, had it succeeded.

Enter Freeman, *booted and spurred.*

Mr. Freeman, your dress commands your welcome to town; what will you drink? I had like to have been imposed upon here by the veriest rascal. 320

FREEMAN.

I am sorry to hear it. The dog flew for't; he had not 'scaped me, if I had been aware of him; Sackbut struck at him but missed his blow, or he had done his business for him.

PERIWINKLE.

I believe you never heard of such a contrivance, Mr. 325 Freeman, as this fellow had found out.

FREEMAN.

Mr. Sackbut has told me the whole story, Mr. Periwinkle. But now I have something to tell you of much more importance to yourself. I happened to lie one night at Coventry, and knowing your uncle, Sir Toby Periwinkle, I paid him a 330 visit and to my great surprise found him dying.

PERIWINKLE.

Dying!

FREEMAN.

Dying, in all appearance; the servants weeping, the room in darkness. The apothecary, shaking his head, told me the

doctors had given him over, and then there is small hopes, 335
you know.

PERIWINKLE.

I hope he has made his will. He always told me he would
make me his heir.

FREEMAN.

I have heard you say as much and therefore resolved to
give you notice. I should think it would not be amiss if you 340
went down tomorrow morning.

PERIWINKLE.

It is a long journey, and the roads very bad.

FREEMAN.

But he has a great estate, and the land very good. Think
upon that.

PERIWINKLE.

Why, that's true, as you say. I'll think upon it. In the mean- 345
time, I give you many thanks for your civility, Mr. Freeman,
and should be glad of your company to dine with me.

FREEMAN.

I am obliged to be at Jonathan's Coffee House at two, and
it is now half an hour after one; if I dispatch my business,
I'll wait on you. I know your hour.   350

PERIWINKLE.

You shall be very welcome, Mr. Freeman; and so, your
humble servant.   *Exit.*

Re-enter Colonel *and* Sackbut.

FREEMAN.

Ha, ha, ha, I have done your business, Colonel; he has
swallowed the bait.

COLONEL.

I overheard all, though I am a little in the dark. I am to 355
personate a highwayman, I suppose. That's a project I am
not fond of; for though I may fright him out of his consent,
he may fright me out of my life when he discovers me, as he
certainly must in the end.

---

348. *Jonathan's Coffee House*] the "general mart of stockjobbers" (*Tatler*,
No. 38); in Exchange Alley, a narrow City street near the Royal Exchange.
358. *he . . . life*] The penalty for highway robbery was death.

FREEMAN.

> No, no, I have a plot for you without danger; but first we   360
> must manage Tradelove. Has the tailor brought your
> clothes?

SACKBUT.

> Yes, pox take the thief.

COLONEL.

> Pox take your drawer for a jolt-headed rogue.

FREEMAN.

> Well, well, no matter; I warrant we have him yet, but now   365
> you must put on the Dutch merchant.

COLONEL.

> The deuce of this trading plot. I wish he had been an old
> soldier, that I might have attacked him in my own way:
> heard him fight over all the battles of the Civil War—but
> for trade, by Jupiter, I shall never do it.   370

SACKBUT.

> Never fear, Colonel, Mr. Freeman will instruct you.

FREEMAN.

> You'll see what others do; the coffee house will instruct
> you.

COLONEL.

> I must venture, however. But I have a farther plot in my
> head upon Tradelove which you must assist me in, Freeman;   375
> you are in credit with him I heard you say.

FREEMAN.

> I am, and will scruple nothing to serve you, Colonel.

COLONEL.

> Come along then. Now for the Dutchman—honest Ptolemy,
> by your leave,
>> Now must bob wig and business come in play,   380
>> And a fair thirty thousand pounder leads the way.

---

364. *jolt-headed*] ?*obs.*, having a clumsy or stupid head.
380. *bob wig*] a simple wig, resembling an actual head of bobbed hair;
perhaps a pun on "bob," *obs.*, verb, "to deceive" or "to make a fool of."

ACT IV

Jonathan's Coffee House in Exchange Alley. Crowd of people with rolls of paper and parchment in their hands; a bar and Coffee Boys *waiting. Enter* Tradelove *and Stockjobbers, with rolls of paper and parchment.*

FIRST STOCKJOBBER.

South Sea at seven-eighths! Who buys?

SECOND STOCKJOBBER.

South Sea bonds due at Michaelmas, 1718! Class Lottery tickets!

THIRD STOCKJOBBER.

East India bonds?

FOURTH STOCKJOBBER.

What, all sellers and no buyers? Gentlemen, I'll buy a   5
thousand pound for Tuesday next at three-fourths.

[A] COFFEE BOY.

Fresh coffee, gentlemen, fresh coffee?

TRADELOVE.

Hark ye, Gabriel, you'll pay the difference of that stock
we transacted for t'other day.

GABRIEL.

Ay, Mr. Tradelove, here's a note for the money, upon the   10
Sword Blade Company.   *Gives him a note.*

[A] COFFEE BOY.

Bohea tea, gentlemen?

6. three-fourths] 3 Fourths *D1–2.*

---

1. *South . . . seven-eighths*] As is usual, only the terminal fraction of the stock's price is quoted. The South Sea Company, established in 1711 to finance the national debt, was a monopoly, trading in Spanish America and the Pacific.

2. *Michaelmas*] September 29, feast of St. Michael.

2–3. *Class Lottery tickets*] one of two continuing state lotteries in which five classes of tickets with corresponding classes of prizes were offered.

10–11. *note . . . Company*] Originally chartered to manufacture hollow sword blades, this company was, in the early eighteenth century, an infamous but powerful banking partnership in Birchin Lane; bankers for the South Sea Company, they also issued paper money that was popular.

12. *Bohea tea*] fine black tea.

Enter a Man.

MAN.

   Is Mr. Smuggle here?

FIRST COFFEE BOY.

   Mr. Smuggle's not here, sir; you'll find him at the books.

SECOND STOCKJOBBER.

   Ho! Here comes two sparks from the other end of the town;   15
   what news bring they?

Enter two Gentlemen.

TRADELOVE.

   I would fain bite that spark in the brown coat; he comes
   very often into the Alley but never employs a broker.

Enter Colonel *and* Freeman.

SECOND STOCKJOBBER.

   Who does anything in the Civil List Lottery? Or Caco?
   —Zounds, where are all the Jews this afternoon?—[*To* Third   20
   Stockjobber.]   Are you a bull or a bear today, Abraham?

THIRD STOCKJOBBER.

   A bull, faith—but I have a good put for next week.

TRADELOVE.

   Mr. Freeman, your servant.   [*Points to the* Colonel.]   Who
   is that gentleman?

FREEMAN.

   A Dutch merchant, just come to England; but hark ye, Mr.   25

15. comes] *D1*; come *D2*.

---

   14. *at the books*] perhaps a reference to gambling rather than accounting;
Eric Partridge glosses *books* as "cards," citing Mrs. Centlivre, but no
specific work, as his authority (*A Dictionary of Slang and Unconventional
English*, 5th ed. [London, 1961]).
   19. *Civil List Lottery*] a state lottery, helping to finance the Civil List,
that is, the royal household.
   19. *Caco*] perhaps a corruption of "cacao," or cocoa beans, a popular
import; or a private lottery, insurance or other joint stock company
(Ca—Co.?); a play on *caco-*, a combining form from Greek, "bad"?
   21. *bull . . . bear*] *bull*: one buying stock, anticipating a rise in price for
later sale; *bear*: one selling stock not yet owned, hoping to buy it for less
than the delivery price.
   22. *put*] "the option of delivering a specified amount of a particular
stock or produce at a certain price within a specified time" (*OED*).

Tradelove—I have a piece of news will get you as much as the French king's death did, if you are expeditious.

TRADELOVE.

Say you so, sir! Pray, what is it?

FREEMAN (*showing him a letter*).

Read there; I received it just now from one that belongs to the emperor's minister.   30

TRADELOVE (*reads [aloud]*).

"Sir, As I have many obligations to you, I cannot miss any opportunity to show my gratitude; this moment, my lord has received a private express that the Spaniards have raised their siege from before Cagliari; if this prove any advantage to you, it will answer both the ends and   35 wishes of, sir, your most obliged humble servant, Henricus Dusseldorp." "Postscript. In two or three hours the news will be public." (*Aside to* Freeman.)   May one depend upon this, Mr. Freeman?

FREEMAN.

You may—I never knew this person send me a false piece   40 of news in my life.

TRADELOVE [*aside to* Freeman].

Sir, I am much obliged to you; egad, 'tis rare news.— [*Aloud.*] Who sells South Sea for next week?

STOCKJOBBERS (*all together*).

I sell; I, I, I, I, I sell.

FIRST STOCKJOBBER.

I'll sell five thousand pounds for next week at five-eighths.   45

SECOND STOCKJOBBER.

I'll sell ten thousand at five-eighths for the same time.

TRADELOVE.

Nay, nay, hold, hold, not all together, gentlemen; I'll be

44. S.D. *all together*] D2; *altogether*   45. five thousand pounds] 5000 *l.*
D1.   D1-2.

47. all together] D2; altogether D1.

26–27. *news . . . did*] Manipulation of the stock market through true and false news reports, often from correspondents, was common practice; cf. I.i.145–150.

33–34. *Spaniards . . . Cagliari*] In the summer of 1717, speculation had arisen over Spain's military preparations. In August, she besieged Cagliari, capital of Sardinia; confusion ensued when Spain falsely promised England and Holland that she would cease the war. However, Freeman's spurious report seems timed before any attack had occurred.

no bull; I'll buy no more than I can take. Will you sell
ten thousand pound at a half, for any day next week except
Saturday?   50

FIRST STOCKJOBBER.
    I'll sell it you, Mr. Tradelove.
                            Freeman *whispers to one of the* Gentlemen.

GENTLEMAN (*aloud*).
    The Spaniards raised the siege of Cagliari! I don't believe
one word of it.

SECOND GENTLEMAN.
    Raised the siege! As much as you have raised the Monument.

FREEMAN.   55
    'Tis raised, I assure you, sir.

SECOND GENTLEMAN.
    What will you lay on't?

FREEMAN.
    What you please.

FIRST GENTLEMAN.
    Why, I have a brother upon the spot in the emperor's
service; I am certain if there were any such thing, I should
have had a letter.   60

A STOCKJOBBER.
    How's this? The siege of Cagliari raised—I wish it may
be true; 'twill make business stir and stocks rise.

FIRST STOCKJOBBER.
    Tradelove's a cunning fat bear; if this news proves true, I
shall repent I sold him the ten thousand pounds.— [*To*
Freeman.] Pray, sir, what assurance have you that the   65
siege is raised?

FREEMAN.
    There is come an express to the emperor's minister.

SECOND STOCKJOBBER.
    I'll know that presently.   *Exit.*

FIRST GENTLEMAN.
    Let it come where it will; I'll hold you fifty pounds 'tis
false.   70

61. S.P. A stockjobber] *D1*; 2d   64. ten] five *D1–2.*
Stock. *D2.*

49–50. *except Saturday*] ironic deference to the Jewish sabbath.
54. *Monument*] a massive columnular structure in Fish Hill Street,
commemorating the Great Fire.

FREEMAN.

'Tis done.

SECOND GENTLEMAN.

I'll lay you a brace of hundreds upon the same.

FREEMAN.

I'll take you.

FOURTH STOCKJOBBER.

Egad, I'll hold twenty pieces 'tis not raised, sir.

FREEMAN.

Done with you, too.   75

TRADELOVE.

I'll lay any man a brace of thousands the siege is
raised.

FREEMAN (*aside to* Tradelove).

The Dutch merchant is your man to take in.

TRADELOVE.

Does not he know the news?

FREEMAN (*to* Tradelove).

Not a syllable; if he did, he would bet a hundred thousand   80
pound as soon as one penny. He's plaguy rich and a mighty
man at wagers.

TRADELOVE.

Say you so—egad, I'll bite him if possible.— [*To the*
Colonel.]   Are you from Holland, sir?

COLONEL.

Ya, mynheer.   85

TRADELOVE.

Had you the news before you came away?

COLONEL.

Wat believe you, mynheer?

TRADELOVE.

What do I believe? Why, I believe that the Spaniards have
actually raised the siege of Cagliari.

COLONEL.

What duyvel's niews is dat? 'Tis niet waer, mynheer—'tis   90
no true, sir.

TRADELOVE.

'Tis so true, mynheer, that I'll lay you two thousand pounds

---

90. *What . . . mynheer*] What devil's news is that? 'Tis not true, sir.

upon it.— [*Aside to* Freeman.] You are sure the letter
may be depended upon, Mr. Freeman?

FREEMAN (*aside to* Tradelove).

Do you think I would venture my money if I were not sure 95
of the truth of it?

COLONEL.

Two duysend pond, mynheer; 'tis gedaen. Dis gentleman
sal hold de gelt. *Gives* Freeman *money.*

FREEMAN.

With all my heart. This binds the wager.

TRADELOVE.

You have certainly lost, mynheer; the siege is raised 100
indeed.

COLONEL.

Ik gelove't niet, Mynheer Freeman; ik sal ye dubbled
houden, if you please.

FREEMAN.

I am let into the secret, therefore won't win your money.

TRADELOVE [*aside*].

Ha, ha, ha! I have snapped the Dutchman, faith, ha, ha. 105
This is no ill day's work.— [*Aloud.*] Pray, may I crave
your name, mynheer?

COLONEL.

Myn naem, mynheer? Myn naem is Jan van Timtamtire-
lereletta Heer van Fainwell.

TRADELOVE.

Zounds, 'tis a damned long name; I shall never remember it. 110
Mynheer van Tim—Tim—Tim—what the devil is it?

FREEMAN.

O, never heed; I know the gentleman and will pass my
word for twice the sum.

TRADELOVE.

That's enough.

99. S.P. FREEMAN] *D1 and D2 assign* *love, using a S.P. for each speech.*
this and the following speech to Trade- 104. won't] *D2;* wont *D1.*

97–98. *Two . . . gelt*] Two thousand pounds, sir; 'tis done. This gentleman shall hold the money.
102–103. *Ik . . . houden*] I don't believe it, sir. I shall hold you doubled.
110. *Zounds*] *rare or obs.,* euphemistic abbreviation of "by God's wounds."

COLONEL (*aside*).

    You'll hear of me sooner than you'll wish, old gentleman, 115
I fancy. —You'll come to Sackbut's, Freeman?

FREEMAN (*aside to the* Colonel).

    Immediately.   *Exit* [Colonel].

FIRST MAN.

    Humphry Hump here?

SECOND [COFFEE] BOY.

    Mr. Humphry Hump is not here; you'll find him upon the
Dutch Walk.   120

TRADELOVE.

    Mr. Freeman, I give you many thanks for your kindness.

FREEMAN (*aside*).

    I fear you'll repent when you know all.

TRADELOVE.

    Will you dine with me?

FREEMAN.

    I am engaged at Sackbut's; adieu.   *Exit.*

TRADELOVE.

    Sir, your humble servant. —Now I'll see what I can do 125
upon Change with my news.   *Exit.*

[IV.ii]   *The tavern.*
                     Enter Freeman *and* Colonel.

FREEMAN.

    Ha, ha, ha! The old fellow swallowed that bait as greedily
as a gudgeon.

COLONEL.

    I have him, faith, ha, ha, ha. His two thousand pound's
secure; if he would keep his money, he must part with
the lady, ha, ha.—What came of your two friends? They   5

---

117. S.D. *Exit* [Colonel] *Exit*   [IV.ii]
follows l. 116 in D1 and D2.   3–4. pound's secure] *D1*; pounds
                        secure *D2.*

---

    120. *Dutch Walk*] Foreign merchants congregated in national groups at
the Royal Exchange (see *Spectator*, No. 69).
    126. *Change*] the Exchange.
[IV.ii]
    2. *gudgeon*] fish used for bait; hence, *fig.*, a gullible person.

performed their part very well; you should have brought
'em to take a glass with us.

FREEMAN.

No matter; we'll drink a bottle together another time. I did
not care to bring them hither; there's no necessity to trust
them with the main secret, you know, Colonel.   10

COLONEL.

Nay, that's right, Freeman.

Enter Sackbut.

SACKBUT.

Joy, joy, Colonel; the luckiest accident in the world!

COLONEL.

What say'st thou?

SACKBUT.

This letter does your business.

COLONEL (*reads* [*aloud*]).

"To Obadiah Prim, hosier, near the building called the   15
Monument, in London."

FREEMAN.

A letter to Prim.— [*To* Sackbut.]   How came you by it?

SACKBUT.

Looking over the letters our postwoman brought, as I
always do to see what letters are directed to my house
(for she can't read, you must know), I spied this, to Prim,   20
so paid for't among the rest; I have given the old jade
a pint of wine on purpose to delay time, till you see
if the letter will be of any service; then I'll seal it up
again and tell her I took it by mistake. I have read it
and fancy you'll like the project—read, read, Colonel.   25

COLONEL (*reads* [*aloud*]).

"Friend Prim, There is arrived from Pennsylvania one
Simon Pure, a leader of the faithful, who hath sojourned
with us eleven days and hath been of great comfort to
the Brethren. He intendeth for the quarterly meeting in
London; I have recommended him to thy house; I pray   30
thee entreat him kindly, and let thy wife cherish him,

---

31. *entreat*] *obs.*, treat.
31. *cherish him*] to treat with tender care; or, *obs.*, to entertain with
kindness.

for he's of weakly constitution. He will depart from
us the third day; which is all from thy friend in the faith,
Aminadab Holdfast." Ha, ha, excellent. I understand
you, landlord, I am to personate this Simon Pure, am I   35
not?

SACKBUT.

Don't you like the hint?

COLONEL.

Admirably well.

FREEMAN.

'Tis the best contrivance in the world, if the right Simon
gets not there before you.   40

COLONEL.

No, no, the Quakers never ride post; he can't be here
before tomorrow at soonest. Do you send and buy me a
Quaker's dress, Mr. Sackbut; and suppose, Freeman, you
should wait at the Bristol coach, that if you see any such
person, you might contrive to give me notice.   45

FREEMAN.

I will. —The country dress and boots, are they ready?

SACKBUT.

Yes, yes, everything, sir.

FREEMAN.

Bring 'em in then.   *Exit* Sackbut.
Thou must dispatch Periwinkle first. Remember, his uncle,
Sir Toby Periwinkle, is an old bachelor of seventy-five,   50
that he has seven hundred a year, most in abbey land; that
he was once in love with your mother, and shrewdly sus-
pected by some to be your father—that you have been
thirty years his steward and ten years his gentleman;
remember to improve these hints.   55

COLONEL.

Never fear; let me alone for that. But what's the steward's
name?

34. Aminadab] Aminidab *D1*;   50. Periwinkle] *D2*; Priwinkle *D1*.
Aminadad *D2*.

---

34. *Aminadab*] a jeering name for a Quaker.
41. *Quakers . . . post*] This most expensive form of transportation was not
suited to Quaker frugality.
51. *abbey land*] land once part of an abbey's estates.

FREEMAN.

His name is Pillage.

COLONEL.

Enough.

Enter Sackbut *with clothes.*

Now for the country put.   *Dresses.*   60

FREEMAN.

Egad, landlord, thou deservest to have the first night's
lodging with the lady for thy fidelity. —What say you,
Colonel, shall we settle a club here, you'll make one?

COLONEL.

Make one? I'll bring a set of honest officers that will spend
their money as freely to their king's health, as they would   65
their blood in his service.

SACKBUT.

I thank you, Colonel.   *(Bell rings.)*   —Here, here.

Exit Sackbut.

COLONEL.

So now for my boots.   *(Puts on boots.)*   Shall I find you
here, Freeman, when I come back?

FREEMAN.

Yes, or I'll leave word with Sackbut where he may send for   70
me. Have you the writings? The will and everything?

COLONEL.

All, all.

Enter Sackbut.

SACKBUT.

Zounds, Mr. Freeman, yonder is Tradelove in the damned'st
passion in the world. He swears you are in the house; he
says you told him you was to dine here.   75

FREEMAN.

I did so, ha, ha, ha. He has found himself bit already.

COLONEL.

The devil! He must not see me in this dress.

SACKBUT [*to* Freeman].

I told him I expected you here but you were not come yet.

65. their king's] *D1*; the king's *D2*.   67. S.D. *Bell rings] follows completed speech in D1 and D2.*

60. *put] obs.* or *arch., slang* or *colloquial,* bumpkin.

FREEMAN.

    Very well. Make you haste out, Colonel, and let me alone
to deal with him. —Where is he?   80

SACKBUT.

    In the King's Head.

COLONEL.

    You remember what I told you?

FREEMAN.

    Ay, ay, very well, landlord; let him know I am come in—
and now, Mr. Pillage, success attend you.   *Exit* Sackbut.

COLONEL.

    Mr. Proteus, rather.—   85

        From changing shape and imitating Jove,
        I draw the happy omens of my love.
        I'm not the first young brother of the blade
        Who made his fortune in a masquerade.

                              Exit Colonel.

                Enter Tradelove.

FREEMAN.

    Zounds, Mr. Tradelove, we're bit, it seems.   90

TRADELOVE.

    Bit, do you call it, Mr. Freeman; I am ruined—pox on
your news.

FREEMAN.

    Pox on the rascal that sent it me.

TRADELOVE.

    Sent it you! Why, Gabriel Skinflint has been at the minister's
and spoke with him, and he has assured him 'tis every   95
syllable false; he received no such express.

FREEMAN.

    I know it. I this minute parted with my friend, who protested
he never sent me any such letter. Some roguish stockjobber has done it on purpose to make me lose my money;
that's certain; I wish I knew who he was; I'd make him 100
repent it. I have lost three hundred pounds by it.

---

    88. *brother of the blade*] cant, soldier; also, brother of Jove, the blade, or
youthful rake.

TRADELOVE.

What signifies your three hundred pounds to what I have
lost? There's two thousand pounds to that Dutchman with
the cursed long name, besides the stock I bought; the
devil! I could tear my flesh. I must never show my face 105
upon Change more, for, by my soul, I can't pay it.

FREEMAN.

I am heartily sorry for't. What can I serve you in? Shall I
speak to the Dutch merchant and try to get you time for
the payment?

TRADELOVE.

Time! Adsheart, I shall never be able to look up again.   110

FREEMAN.

I am very much concerned that I was the occasion and wish
I could be an instrument of retrieving your misfortune;
for my own, I value it not. —Adso! A thought comes into
my head that, well improved, may be of service.

TRADELOVE.

Ah, there's no thought can be of any service to me without 115
paying the money, or running away.

FREEMAN.

How do you know? What do you think of my proposing
Mrs. Lovely to him? He is a single man, and I heard him
say he had a mind to marry an English woman; nay, more
than that, he said somebody told him you had a pretty ward. 120
He wished you had betted her instead of your money.

TRADELOVE.

Ay, but he'd be hanged before he'd take her instead of the
money; the Dutch are too covetous for that; besides, he did
not know that there were three more of us, I suppose.

FREEMAN.

So much the better; you may venture to give him your con- 125
sent, if he'll forgive you the wager. It is not your business
to tell him that your consent will signify nothing.

102. three hundred pounds] 300 *l.*
D1–2.

_____

110. *Adsheart*] *Ads*, variant of "Ods," minced form of "God's"; "God's
heart."
113. *Adso*] variant of "Odso."

TRADELOVE.

That's right, as you say; but will he do it, think you?

FREEMAN.

I can't tell that; but I'll try what I can do with him. He has promised me to meet me here an hour hence; I'll feel 130 his pulse and let you know. If I find it feasible, I'll send for you; if not, you are at liberty to take what measures you please.

TRADELOVE.

You must extol her beauty, double her portion, and tell him I have the entire disposal of her, and that she can't marry 135 without my consent—and that I am a covetous rogue and will never part with her without a valuable consideration.

FREEMAN.

Ay, ay, let me alone for a lie at a pinch.

TRADELOVE.

Egad, if you can bring this to bear, Mr. Freeman, I'll make you whole again; I'll pay the three hundred pounds you 140 lost, with all my soul.

FREEMAN.

Well, I'll use my best endeavors. Where will you be?

TRADELOVE.

At home; pray Heaven you prosper. If I were but the sole trustee now, I should not fear it. Who the devil would be a guardian, 145
　　　If when cash runs low, our coffers t'enlarge,
　　　　　We can't, like other stocks, transfer our charge? *Exit.*

FREEMAN.

Ha, ha, ha, he has it! *Exit.*

[IV.iii]　　　　　　*Periwinkle's house.*
Enter Periwinkle *on one side and* Footman *on t'other.*

FOOTMAN.

A gentleman from Coventry inquires for you, sir.

PERIWINKLE.

From my uncle, I warrant you; bring him up.

[*Exit* Footman.]

This will save me the trouble as well as the expenses of a journey.

Enter Colonel.

COLONEL.

Is your name Periwinkle, sir?   5

PERIWINKLE.

It is, sir.

COLONEL.

I am sorry for the message I bring. My old master, whom I served these forty years, claims the sorrow due from a faithful servant to an indulgent master.   *Weeps.*

PERIWINKLE.

By this I understand, sir, my uncle, Sir Toby Periwinkle,   10
is dead.

COLONEL.

He is, sir, and he has left you heir to seven hundred a year, in as good abbey land as ever paid Peter pence to Rome. I wish you long to enjoy it, but my tears will flow when I think of my benefactor. (*Weeps.*) Ah, he was a   15
good man; he has not left many of his fellows. The poor laments him sorely.

PERIWINKLE.

I pray, sir, what office bore you?

COLONEL.

I was his steward, sir.

PERIWINKLE.

I have heard him mention you with much respect; your   20
name is—

COLONEL.

Pillage, sir.

PERIWINKLE.

Ay, Pillage. I do remember he called you Pillage. Pray, Mr. Pillage, when did my uncle die?

COLONEL.

Monday last at four in the morning. About two, he signed   25
this will and gave it into my hands and strictly charged

---

13. *Peter pence*] an annual penny tax paid by English households before the Reformation to the papal see in Rome on St. Peter's day.

me to leave Coventry the moment he expired, and deliver
it to you with what speed I could. I have obeyed him, sir,
and there is the will.   *Gives it to* Periwinkle.

PERIWINKLE.

'Tis very well; I'll lodge it in the Commons.   30

COLONEL.

There are two things which he forgot to insert but
charged me to tell you that he desired you'd perform them as
readily as if you had found them written in the will, which
is to remove his corpse and bury him by his father in St.
Paul-Covent-Garden, and to give all his servants mourning.   35

PERIWINKLE (*aside*).

That will be a considerable charge; a pox of all modern
fashions.— [*Aloud.*]   Well, it shall be done, Mr. Pillage;
I will agree with one of death's fashion mongers, called an
undertaker, to go down and bring up the body.

COLONEL.

I hope, sir, I shall have the honor to serve you in the   40
same station I did your worthy uncle; I have not many
years to stay behind him and would gladly spend them in the
family where I was brought up.   (*Weeps.*)   He was a kind
and tender master to me.

PERIWINKLE.

Pray, don't grieve, Mr. Pillage; you shall hold your place   45
and everything else which held under my uncle. You
make me weep to see you so concerned.   (*Weeps.*)   He
lived to a good old age, and we are all mortal.

COLONEL.

We are so, sir, and therefore I must beg you to sign this
lease. You'll find Sir Toby has ta'en particular notice   50
of it in his will. I could not get it time enough from the
lawyer, or he had signed it before he died.

                                        Gives him a paper.

PERIWINKLE.

A lease for what?

COLONEL.

I rented a hundred a year of Sir Toby upon lease, which

34–35. *St. Paul-Covent-Garden*] St. Paul's, Covent Garden, a fashionable
church, designed by Inigo Jones, on the west side of Covent Garden
Square.

lease expires at Lady Day next, and I desire to renew it   55
for twenty years; that's all, sir.

PERIWINKLE.

    Let me see.   *Looks over the lease.*

COLONEL *(aside)*.

    Matters go swimmingly, if nothing intervene.

PERIWINKLE.

    Very well, let's see what he says in his will about it.
        Lays the lease upon the table and looks on the will.

COLONEL *(aside)*.

    He's very wary, yet I fancy I shall be too cunning for him.   60

PERIWINKLE.

    Ho, here it is—"the farm lying . . . now in possession of
Samuel Pillage . . . suffer him to renew his lease . . . at the
same rent . . . ." Very well, Mr. Pillage, I see my uncle
does mention it, and I'll perform his will. Give me the
lease. (Colonel *gives it him; he looks upon it and lays it*   65
upon the table.) Pray you, step to the door and call for a
pen and ink, Mr. Pillage.

COLONEL.

    I have pen and ink in my pocket, sir.   *(Pulls out an inkhorn.)*
I never go without that.

PERIWINKLE.

    I think it belongs to your profession.   70

He looks upon the pen while the Colonel *changes the lease and lays down the
contract.*

    I doubt this is but a sorry pen, though it may serve to
write my name.   *Writes.*

COLONEL *(aside)*.

    Little does he think what he signs.

PERIWINKLE.

    There is your lease, Mr. Pillage.   *(Gives him the paper.)*
Now I must desire you to make what haste you can down to   75
Coventry and take care of everything, and I'll send down
the undertaker for the body; do you attend it up, and
whatever charge you are at, I will repay you.

---

55. *Lady Day*] March 25, feast of the Annunciation and the spring
quarter day.

COLONEL (*aside*).

    You have paid me already, I thank you, sir.

PERIWINKLE.

    Will you dine with me?   80

COLONEL.

    I would rather not; there are some of my neighbors which
I met as I came along, who leaves the town this afternoon,
they told me, and I should be glad of their company down.

PERIWINKLE.

    Well, well, I won't detain you.

COLONEL (*aside*).

    I don't care how soon I am out.   85

PERIWINKLE.

    I will give orders about mourning.

COLONEL [*aside*].

    You will have cause to mourn, when you know your estate
imaginary only.

        You'll find your hopes and cares alike are vain.

        In spite of all the caution you have ta'en.   90

        Fortune rewards the faithful lover's pain.   *Exit.*

PERIWINKLE.

    Seven hundred a year! I wish he had died seventeen years
ago. What a valuable collection of rarities might I have
had by this time! I might have traveled over all the
known parts of the globe and made my own closet rival the 95
Vatican at Rome. —Odso, I have a good mind to begin my
travels now. Let me see—I am but sixty. My father,
grandfather, and great-grandfather reached ninety odd. I
have almost forty years good. —Let me consider—what
will seven hundred a year amount to—in—ay, in thirty 100
years; I'll say but thirty. Thirty times seven is seven
times thirty—that is—just twenty-one thousand pound.
'Tis a great deal of money. I may very well reserve sixteen
hundred of it for a collection of such rarities as will
make my name famous to posterity. I would not die like 105
other mortals, forgotten in a year or two, as my uncle will
be—no.

        With nature's curious works I'll raise my fame,

        That men, till doomsday, may repeat my name.   *Exit.*

91. rewards] *D1b–2*; reward *D1a*.

[IV.iv]   *A tavern.*
                   Freeman *and* Tradelove *over a bottle.*

TRADELOVE.

Come, Mr. Freeman, here's Mynheer Jan van Tim—Tam—
Tam—I shall never think of that Dutchman's name.

FREEMAN.

Mynheer Jan van Timtamtirelireletta Heer van Fainwell.

TRADELOVE.

Ay, Heer van Fainwell; I never heard such a confounded
name in my life. Here's his health, I say.   *Drinks.*   5

FREEMAN.

With all my heart.

TRADELOVE.

Faith, I never expected to have found so generous a thing
in a Dutchman.

FREEMAN.

O, he has nothing of the Hollander in his temper, except
an antipathy to monarchy. As soon as I told him your   10
circumstances, he replied he would not be the ruin of
any man for the world and immediately made this proposal
himself: "Let him take what time he will for the payment,"
said he, "or if he'll give me his ward, I'll forgive him the
debt."   15

TRADELOVE.

Well, Mr. Freeman, I can but thank you. Egad, you have
made a man of me again; and if ever I lay a wager more,
may I rot in a jail.

FREEMAN.

I assure you, Mr. Tradelove, I was very much concerned
because I was the occasion—though very innocently, I   20
protest.

TRADELOVE.

I dare swear you was, Mr. Freeman.

                   Enter a Fiddler [*with his* Wife].

FIDDLER.

Please to have a lesson of music or a song, gentlemen?

18. jail] goal *D1–2.*

---

10. *antipathy to monarchy*] After the Dutch rebelled against Spain in the
sixteenth century, they formed a republic; it was not functioning efficiently
in 1718.

FREEMAN.

A song, ay, with all our hearts; have you ever a merry one?

FIDDLER.

Yes, sir, my wife and I can give you a merry dialogue.   25

Here is the song.

TRADELOVE.

'Tis very pretty, faith.

FREEMAN.

There's something for you to drink, friend; go, lose no time.

FIDDLER.

I thank you, sir.   *Exeunt.*

Enter Drawer and Colonel, *dressed for the Dutch Merchant.*

COLONEL.

Ha, Mynheer Tradelove, ik ben sorry voor your troubles—   30
maer ik sal you easy maeken; ik wil de gelt niet hebben.

TRADELOVE.

I shall forever acknowledge the obligation, sir.

FREEMAN.

But you understand upon what condition, Mr. Tradelove:
Mrs. Lovely.

COLONEL.

Ya, de juffrow sal al te regt setten, mynheer.   35

TRADELOVE.

With all my heart, mynheer, you shall have my consent to
marry her freely.

FREEMAN.

Well then, as I am a party concerned between you, Mynheer
Jan van Timtamtirelireletta Heer van Fainwell shall give
you a discharge of your wager under his own hand, and   40
you shall give him your consent to marry Mrs. Lovely
under yours. That is the way to avoid all manner of disputes
hereafter.

---

29. S.D. *Exeunt*] *Exit D1–2.*   31. de gelt] degelt *D1–2.*

---

25. *dialogue*] a conversational song for two or more voices.
30–31. *ik . . . hebben*] I am sorry for your troubles—but I shall make you
easy; I will not have the money.
35. *Ya . . . mynheer*] Yes, the lady shall set all to rights, sir.

COLONEL.

Ya, waeragtig.

TRADELOVE.

Ay, ay, so it is, Mr. Freeman; I'll give it under mine this   45
minute.   *Sits down to write.*

COLONEL.

And so sal ik.   *Sits down to write.*

FREEMAN.

Soho, the house!

Enter Drawer.

Bid your master come up.— (*Aside.*)   I'll see there be
witnesses enough to the bargain.   [*Exit Drawer.*]   50

Enter Sackbut.

SACKBUT.

Do you call, gentlemen?

FREEMAN.

Ay, Mr. Sackbut, we shall want your hand here.

TRADELOVE.

There, mynheer, there's my consent as amply as you can
desire; but you must insert your own name, for I know not
how to spell it; I have left a blank for it.   55
                              Gives the Colonel *a paper.*

COLONEL.

Ya, ik sal dat well doen.

FREEMAN.

Now, Mr. Sackbut, you and I will witness it.   *They write.*

COLONEL.

Daer, Mynheer Tradelove, is your discharge.   *Gives him a paper*

TRADELOVE.

Be pleased to witness this receipt too, gentlemen.
                      Freeman *and* Sackbut *put their hands.*

FREEMAN.

Ay, ay, that we will.   60

---

48. Soho] So, ho *D1–2.*

---

44. *Ya, waeragtig*] Yes, truly.
56. *Ya . . . doen*] Yes, I shall do that well.

COLONEL.

Well, mynheer, ye most meer doen; ye most myn voorspraek
to de juffrow syn.

FREEMAN.

He means you must recommend him to the lady.

TRADELOVE.

That I will, and to the rest of my brother guardians.

COLONEL.

Wat voor den duyvel, heb you meer guardians?   65

TRADELOVE.

Only three, mynheer.

COLONEL.

Wat, donder heb ye myn betrocken, mynheer? Had ik that
gewoeten, ik soude eaven met you geweest syn.

SACKBUT.

But Mr. Tradelove is the principal, and he can do a great
deal with the rest, sir.   70

FREEMAN.

And he shall use his interest, I promise you, mynheer.

TRADELOVE.

I will say all that ever I can think on to recommend you,
mynheer; and if you please, I'll introduce you to the lady.

COLONEL.

Well, dat is waer. Maer ye must first spreken of myn to de
juffrow, and to de oudere, gentlemen.   75

FREEMAN.

Ay, that's the best way, and then I and the Heer van
Fainwell will meet you there.

TRADELOVE.

I will go this moment, upon honor. Your most obedient
humble servant.— [Aside.]   My speaking will do you little

75. oudere, gentlemen] *D1*; oudere
gentlemen *D2*.

61–62. *ye . . . syn*] you must do more; you must speak well of me to the
lady.

65. *Wat . . . guardians*] What the devil, have you more guardians?

67–68. *Wat . . . syn*] What, then you have tricked me, sir? Had I known
that, I would have been even with you.

74–75. *dat . . . oudere*] that is certain. But first you must speak to the lady
about me, and to the parents [guardians].

good, mynheer, ha, ha; we have bit you, faith, ha, ha; my   80
debt's discharged, and for the man,
        He's my consent—to get her if he can.   *Exit.*

COLONEL.

Ha, ha, ha, this was a masterpiece of contrivance, Freeman.

FREEMAN.

He hugs himself with his supposed good fortune and
little thinks the luck's of our side. But come, pursue the   85
fickle goddess while she's in the mood. Now for the Quaker.

COLONEL.

That's the hardest task.
        Of all the counterfeits performed by man,
        A soldier makes the simplest Puritan.   *Exit.*

82. He's my] *D1*; He'as my *D2*.   *in D1.*
This line is treated as verse in D2 but not

---

 84. *hugs himself*] *fig.*, congratulates himself.

ACT V

Prim's house.
Enter Mrs. Prim *and* Mrs. Lovely *in Quaker's dress, meeting.*

MRS. PRIM.

So now I like thee, Ann. Art thou not better without thy
monstrous hoop coat and patches? If Heaven should
make thee so many black spots upon thy face, would it not
fright thee, Ann?

MRS. LOVELY.

If it should turn your inside outward and show all the   5
spots of your hypocrisy, 'twould fright me worse.

MRS. PRIM.

My hypocrisy! I scorn thy words, Ann; I lay no baits.

MRS. LOVELY.

If you did, you'd catch no fish.

MRS. PRIM.

Well, well, make thy jests, but I'd have thee to know,
Ann, that I could have catched as many fish (as thou   10
call'st them) in my time as ever thou didst with all thy
fool traps about thee. If admirers be thy aim, thou wilt
have more of them in this dress than thy other. The men,
take my word for't, are most desirous to see what we are
most careful to conceal.   15

MRS. LOVELY.

Is that the reason of your formality, Mrs. Prim? Truth
will out. I ever thought, indeed, there was more design
than godliness in the pinched cap.

MRS. PRIM.

Go, thou art corrupted with reading lewd plays and filthy
romances, good for nothing but to lead youth into the   20
high road of fornication. Ah! I wish thou art not already
too familiar with the wicked ones.

MRS. LOVELY.

Too familiar with the wicked ones! Pray, no more of those
freedoms, madam; I am familiar with none so wicked as

17. more] *D1*; no more *D2*.

---

2. *patches*] artificial beauty spots made of cloth or paper.

yourself. How dare you talk thus to me. You, you, you   25
unworthy woman, you—   *Bursts into tears.*

Enter Tradelove.

TRADELOVE.

What, in tears, Nancy?—What have you done to her, Mrs.
Prim, to make her weep?

MRS. LOVELY.

Done to me! I admire I keep my senses among you. But
I will rid myself of your tyranny if there be either law   30
or justice to be had. I'll force you to give me up my
liberty.

MRS. PRIM.

Thou hast more need to weep for thy sins, Ann—yea, for
thy manifold sins.

MRS. LOVELY.

Don't think that I'll be still the fool which you have made   35
me. No, I'll wear what I please, go when and where I
please, and keep what company I think fit, and not what
you shall direct—I will.

TRADELOVE.

For my part, I do think all this very reasonable, Mrs.
Lovely. 'Tis fit you should have your liberty, and for   40
that very purpose I am come.

Enter Mr. Periwinkle *and* Obadiah Prim *with a letter in his hand.*

PERIWINKLE.

I have bought some black stockings of your husband, Mrs.
Prim, but he tells me the glover's trade belongs to you;
therefore, I pray you look me out five or six dozen of
mourning gloves, such as are given at funerals, and send   45
them to my house.

PRIM.

My friend Periwinkle has got a good windfall today—
seven hundred a year.

MRS. PRIM.

I wish thee joy of it, neighbor.

42. stockings] *D2*; stockins *D1*.

TRADELOVE.

What, is Sir Toby dead then?   50

PERIWINKLE.

He is. —You'll take care, Mrs. Prim?

MRS. PRIM.

Yea, I will, neighbor.

PRIM [*to* Mrs. Prim].

This letter recommendeth a speaker; 'tis from Aminadab Holdfast of Bristol; peradventure he will be here
this night; therefore, Sarah, do thou take care for his   55
reception.   *Gives her the letter.*

MRS. PRIM.

I will obey thee.   *Exit.*

PRIM.

What are thou in the dumps for, Ann?

TRADELOVE.

We must marry her, Mr. Prim.

PRIM.

Why truly, if we could find a husband worth having, I   60
should be as glad to see her married as thou wouldst,
neighbor.

PERIWINKLE.

Well said; there are but few worth having.

TRADELOVE.

I can recommend you a man now that I think you can
none of you have an objection to.   65

Enter Sir Philip Modelove.

PERIWINKLE.

You recommend! Nay, whenever she marries, I'll recommend the husband.

SIR PHILIP.

What must it be, a whale or a rhinoceros, Mr. Periwinkle,
ha, ha, ha? —Mr. Tradelove, I have a bill upon you (*gives
him a paper*), and have been seeking for you all over the   70
town.

65. to] *D2*; too *D1*.

---

53. *speaker*] the head of a convocation house or synod.
69. *bill*] bill of exchange, a money order with a due date, used to avoid
transmitting cash in long distance trading.

TRADELOVE.

I'll accept it, Sir Philip, and pay it when due.

PERIWINKLE.

He shall be none of the fops at your end of the town with full perukes and empty skulls, nor yet none of your trading gentry, who puzzle the heralds to find arms for their coaches. No, he shall be a man famous for travels, solidity, and curiosity—one who has searched into the profundity of nature. When Heaven shall direct such a one, he shall have my consent, because it may turn to the benefit of mankind.

MRS. LOVELY.

The benefit of mankind! What, would you anatomize me?

SIR PHILIP.

Ay, ay, madam, he would dissect you.

TRADELOVE.

Or pore over you through a microscope to see how your blood circulates from the crown of your head to the sole of your foot, ha, ha! But I have a husband for you, a man that knows how to improve your fortune; one that trades to the four corners of the globe.

MRS. LOVELY.

And would send me for a venture, perhaps.

TRADELOVE.

One that will dress you in all the pride of Europe, Asia, Africa, and America—a Dutch merchant, my girl.

SIR PHILIP.

A Dutchman! Ha, ha, there's a husband for a fine lady— ya juffrow, will you met myn slapen—ha, ha. He'll learn you to talk the language of the hogs, madam, ha, ha.

TRADELOVE.

He'll learn you that one merchant is of more service to a nation than fifty coxcombs. The Dutch know the trading interest to be of more benefit to the state than the landed.

SIR PHILIP.

But what is either interest to a lady?

83–84. *microscope . . . circulates*] The recent invention of the microscope aided scientists in studying the blood circulation.

92. *ya . . . slapen*] yes, lady, will you sleep with me?

TRADELOVE.

'Tis the merchant makes the belle. How would the ladies
sparkle in the box without the merchant? The Indian 100
diamonds! The French brocade! The Italian fan! The
Flanders lace! The fine Dutch holland! How would they vent
their scandal over their tea tables? And where would you
beaus have champagne to toast your mistresses, were it not
for the merchant? 105

PRIM.

Verily, neighbor Tradelove, thou dost waste thy breath
about nothing. All that thou hast said tendeth only to de-
bauch youth and fill their heads with the price and luxury
of this world. The merchant is a very great friend to Satan
and sendeth as many to his dominions as the pope. 110

PERIWINKLE.

Right, I say knowledge makes the man.

PRIM.

Yea, but not thy kind of knowledge. It is the knowledge
of truth. Search thou for the light within and not for
baubles, friend.

MRS. LOVELY.

Ah, study your country's good, Mr. Periwinkle, and not 115
her insects; rid you of your home-bred monsters before you
fetch any from abroad. I dare swear you have maggots
enough in your own brain to stock all the virtuosos in
Europe with butterflies.

SIR PHILIP.

By my soul, Miss Nancy's a wit. 120

PRIM.

That is more than she can say by thee, friend. Look ye,
it is in vain to talk; when I meet a man worthy of her,
she shall have my leave to marry him.

MRS. LOVELY.

Provided he be one of the faithful.— (*Aside.*) Was there
ever such a swarm of caterpillars to blast the hopes of 125
a woman?— [*Aloud.*] Know this: that you contend in vain.
I'll have no husband of your choosing, nor shall you lord

---

113. *light within*] the inner conscience and self-scrutiny that Quakers
deemed necessary guides towards godliness.

it over me long. I'll try the power of an English senate—
orphans have been redressed and wills set aside, and none
did ever deserve their pity more.— [*Aside.*]   O Fainwell! 130
Where are thy promises to free me from these vermin?
Alas, the task was more difficult than he imagined!

> A harder task than what the poets tell
> Of yore, the fair Andromeda befell;
> She but one monster feared, I've four to fear,   135
> And see no Perseus, no deliv'rer near.   *Exit.*

Enter Servant *and whispers to* Prim.

SERVANT.

One Simon Pure inquireth for thee.   [*Exit.*]

PERIWINKLE.

The woman is mad.   *Exit.*

SIR PHILIP.

So are you all, in my opinion.   *Exit.*

PRIM.

Friend Tradelove, business requireth my presence.   140

TRADELOVE.

O, I shan't trouble you.— [*Aside.*]   Pox take him for an
unmannerly dog—however, I have kept my word with my
Dutchman and will introduce him too for all you.   *Exit.*

Enter Colonel *in a Quaker's habit.*

PRIM.

Friend Pure, thou art welcome; how is it with Friend
Holdfast and all Friends in Bristol? Timothy Littlewit, 145
John Slenderbrain, and Christopher Keepfaith?

COLONEL (*aside.*)

A goodly company!— [*Aloud.*]   They are all in health, I
thank thee for them.

PRIM.

Friend Holdfast writes me word that thou camest lately
from Pennsylvania; how do all Friends there?   150

COLONEL (*aside*).

What the devil shall I say? I know just as much of Pennsylvania as I do of Bristol.

PRIM.

Do they thrive?

COLONEL.

Yea, friend, the blessing of their good works fall upon them.   155

Enter Mrs. Prim *and* Mrs. Lovely.

PRIM.

Sarah, know our Friend Pure.

MRS. PRIM.

Thou art welcome.   *He salutes her.*

COLONEL (*aside*).

Here comes the sum of all my wishes. How charming she appears, even in that disguise.

PRIM.

Why dost thou consider the maiden so intentively, friend?   160

COLONEL.

I will tell thee. About four days ago, I saw a vision—this very maiden, but in vain attire, standing on a precipice; and heard a voice, which called me by my name and bade me put forth my hand and save her from the pit. I did so, and methought the damsel grew to my side.   165

MRS. PRIM.

What can that portend?

PRIM.

The damsel's conversion, I am persuaded.

MRS. LOVELY (*aside*).

That's false, I'm sure.

PRIM.

Wilt thou use the means, Friend Pure?

COLONEL.

Means! What means? Is she not thy daughter and already   170
one of the faithful?

MRS. PRIM.

No, alas. She's one of the ungodly.

PRIM [*to* Mrs. Lovely].

Pray thee, mind what this good man will say unto thee; he will teach thee the way that thou shouldest walk, Ann.

---

165. damsel] damosel *D1–2*   *of the text*).
(*silently regularized throughout the rest*

---

174. *way . . . walk*] *fig.*, chiefly religious, how to conduct oneself with piety.

MRS. LOVELY.

I know my way without his instructions. I hoped to have 175
been quiet when once I had put on your odious formality
here.

COLONEL.

Then thou wearest it out of compulsion, not choice,
friend?

MRS. LOVELY.

Thou art in the right of it, friend.   180

MRS. PRIM.

Art not thou ashamed to mimic the good man? Ah, thou
art a stubborn girl.

COLONEL.

Mind her not; she hurteth not me. If thou wilt leave her
alone with me, I will discuss some few points with her that
may, perchance, soften her stubbornness and melt her into 185
compliance.

PRIM.

Content; I pray thee put it home to her. —Come, Sarah,
let us leave the good man with her.

[Mrs. Lovely] *catching hold of* Prim; *he breaks loose and exit* [*with*
Mrs. Prim].

MRS. LOVELY [*calls after them*].

What do you mean—to leave me with this old enthusiastical
canter? Don't think, because I complied with your formality, 190
to impose your ridiculous doctrine upon me.

COLONEL.

I pray thee, young woman, moderate thy passion.

MRS. LOVELY.

I pray thee, walk after thy leader; you will but lose your
labor upon me. —These wretches will certainly make me
mad.   195

COLONEL.

I am of another opinion; the spirit telleth me that I shall
convert thee, Ann.

MRS. LOVELY.

'Tis a lying spirit; don't believe it.

COLONEL.

Say'st thou so? Why, then thou shalt convert me, my angel.

Catching her in his arms.

–83–

MRS. LOVELY (*shrieks*).

 Ah! Monster, hold off, or I'll tear thy eyes out.   200

COLONEL [*whispers*].

 Hush! For Heaven's sake—dost thou know me? I am
Fainwell.

MRS. LOVELY.

 Fainwell!

Enter old Prim.

 (*Aside.*) O, I'm undone; Prim here—I wish with all my
soul I had been dumb.   205

PRIM.

 What is the matter? Why didst thou shriek out, Ann?

MRS. LOVELY.

 Shriek out! I'll shriek and shriek again, cry murder,
thieves, or anything to drown the noise of that eternal
babbler, if you leave me with him any longer.

PRIM.

 Was that all? Fie, fie, Ann.   210

COLONEL.

 No matter; I'll bring down her stomach, I'll warrant thee.
Leave us, I pray thee.

PRIM.

 Fare thee well.   *Exit.*

COLONEL.

 My charming lovely woman.   *Embraces her.*

MRS. LOVELY.

 What means thou by this disguise, Fainwell?   215

COLONEL.

 To set thee free, if thou wilt perform thy promise.

MRS. LOVELY.

 Make me mistress of my fortune, and make thy own
conditions.

COLONEL.

 This night shall answer all thy wishes. See here, I have
the consent of three of thy guardians already, and doubt 220
not but Prim shall make the fourth.

[*Door opens slightly, unobserved,*] Prim *listening.*

201. thou know] *D1*; thou not 215. means] *D1*; mean'st *D2.*
know *D2.*

---

 211. *stomach*] *obs.*, anger.

PRIM (*aside*).

I would gladly hear what argument the good man useth to bend her.

MRS. LOVELY [*unaware of* Prim].

Thy words give me new life, methinks.

PRIM [*aside*].

What do I hear? 225

MRS. LOVELY [*still unaware of* Prim].

Thou best of men! Heaven meant to bless me sure, when first I saw thee.

PRIM [*aside*].

He hath mollified her. O wonderful conversion!

COLONEL [*sees* Prim; *aside to* Mrs. Lovely].

Ha! Prim listening—no more, my love; we are observed; seem to be edified, and give 'em hopes that thou wilt turn 230 Quaker, and leave the rest to me.— (*Aloud.*)   I am glad to find that thou art touched with what I said unto thee, Ann; another time I will explain the other article to thee. In the meanwhile be thou dutiful to our Friend Prim.

MRS. LOVELY.

I shall obey thee in everything. 235

Enter old Prim.

PRIM.

O, what a prodigious change is here! Thou hast wrought a miracle, friend! Ann, how dost thou like the doctrine he hath preached?

MRS. LOVELY.

So well that I could talk to him forever, methinks. I am ashamed of my former folly and ask your pardon, Mr. Prim. 240

COLONEL.

Enough, enough that thou art sorry; he is no pope, Ann.

PRIM.

Verily, thou dost rejoice me exceedingly, friend; will it please thee to walk into the next room and refresh thyself? Come, take the maiden by the hand.

COLONEL.

We will follow thee. 245

Enter Servant.

SERVANT.

There is another Simon Pure inquireth for thee, master.

COLONEL (*aside*).

> The devil there is.

PRIM.

> Another Simon Pure? I do not know him; is he any relation
> of thine?

COLONEL.

> No, friend, I know him not.— (*Aside.*)   Pox take him; I 250
> wish he were in Pennsylvania again, with all my blood.

MRS. LOVELY (*aside*).

> What shall I do?

PRIM [*to* Servant].

> Bring him up.   [*Exit* Servant.]

COLONEL [*aside*].

> Humph, then one of us must go down; that's certain. Now
> impudence assist me.   255

Enter Simon Pure.

PRIM.

> What is thy will with me, friend?

PURE.

> Didst thou not receive a letter from Aminadab Holdfast
> of Bristol, concerning one Simon Pure?

PRIM.

> Yea, and Simon Pure is already here, friend.

COLONEL (*aside*).

> And Simon Pure will stay here, friend, if possible.   260

PURE.

> That's an untruth, for I am he.

COLONEL.

> Take thou heed, friend, what thou dost say; I do affirm
> that I am Simon Pure.

PURE.

> Thy name may be Pure, friend, but not that Pure.

COLONEL.

> Yea, that Pure which my good Friend Aminadab Holdfast 265
> wrote to my Friend Prim about, the same Simon Pure that
> came from Pennsylvania and sojourned in Bristol eleven
> days; thou wouldst not take my name from me, wouldst
> thou?— (*Aside.*)   Till I have done with it.

PURE.

> Thy name! I am astounded.   270

COLONEL.

At what? At thy own assurance?

Going up to him; S. Pure *starts back.*

PURE.

Avaunt, Satan; approach me not! I defy thee and all thy works.

MRS. LOVELY (*aside*).

O, he'll outcant him—undone, undone forever.

COLONEL.

Hark thee, friend, thy sham will not take. Don't exert 275 thy voice; thou art too well acquainted with Satan to start at him, thou wicked reprobate. What can thy design be here?

Enter Servant and gives Prim *a letter.*

PRIM.

One of these must be a counterfeit, but which I cannot say.

[*Exit Servant.*]

COLONEL (*aside*).

What can that letter be?   [Prim *reads the letter.*] 280

PURE.

Thou must be the devil, friend; that's certain, for no human power can stock so great a falsehood.

PRIM [*to* S. Pure].

This letter sayeth that thou art better acquainted with that Prince of Darkness than any here. —Read that, I pray thee, Simon.   *Gives it the* Colonel. 285

COLONEL [*aside*].

'Tis Freeman's hand.— (*Reads* [*aloud*].) "There is a design formed to rob your house this night and cut your throat, and for that purpose there is a man disguised like a Quaker who is to pass for one Simon Pure; the gang whereof I am one, though now resolved to rob no more, has been at 290 Bristol; one of them came up in the coach with the Quaker, whose name he hath taken, and from what he gathered from him, formed that design and did not doubt but he

292. he gathered] *D1*; he hath gathered *D2.*

272. *Avaunt*] *interjection*, begone.

should impose so far upon you as to make you turn out the
real Simon Pure and keep him with you. Make the right 295
use of this. Adieu."— (*Aside.*)   Excellent well!

PRIM (*to* S. Pure).

Dost thou hear this?

PURE.

Yea, but it moveth me not; that, doubtless, is the impostor.   *Pointing at the* Colonel.

COLONEL.

Ah, thou wicked one! Now I consider thy face, I remember 300
thou didst come up in the leathern convenience with me;
thou hadst a black bob wig on and a brown camblet coat
with brass buttons. Canst thou deny it, ha?

PURE.

Yea, I can and with a safe conscience too, friend.

PRIM.

Verily, friend, thou art the most impudent villain I ever 305
saw.

MRS. LOVELY (*aside*).

Nay then, I'll have a fling at him too.— [*Aloud.*]   I
remember the ·face of this fellow at Bath—ay, this is he
that picked my Lady Raffle's pocket upon the grove;
don't you remember that the mob pumped you, friend? 310
This is the most notorious rogue—

PURE.

What doth provoke thee to seek my life? Thou wilt not
hang me, wilt thou, wrongfully?

PRIM.

She will do thee no hurt, nor thou shalt do me none; therefore, get thee about thy business, friend, and leave thy 315
wicked course of life, or thou mayst not come off so favorably
everywhere.

307. him too] *D1*; him *D2*.

---

301. *leathern convenience*] a circumlocution for "coach," attributed to
Quakers and used derisively.

302. *camblet*] variant of "camlet," an expensive oriental fabric, usually
made from Angora goat fleece.

310. *pumped you*] ?*obs.*, in medical therapy, to put someone under water
emitted by a pump; a reference to the spa at Bath.

COLONEL.

Go, friend, I would advise thee, and tempt thy fate no more.

PURE.

Yea, I will go, but it shall be to thy confusion; for I shall clear myself. I will return with some proofs that shall 320 convince thee, Obadiah, that thou art highly imposed upon.   *Exit.*

COLONEL (*aside*).

Then here will be no staying for me, that's certain. What the devil shall I do?

PRIM.

What monstrous works of iniquity are there in this world, 325 Simon.

COLONEL.

Yea, the age is full of vice.— (*Aside.*) 'Sdeath, I am so confounded I know not what to say.

PRIM.

Thou art disordered, friend; art thou not well?

COLONEL.

My spirit is greatly troubled, and something telleth me that 330 though I have wrought a good work in converting this maiden, this tender maiden, yet my labor will be in vain; for the evil spirit fighteth against her; and I see, yea, I see with the eyes of my inward man that Satan will rebuffet her again whenever I withdraw myself from her; and she will, yea, 335 this very damsel will return again to that abomination from whence I have retrieved her, as if it were, yea, as if it were out of the jaws of the fiend—hum—

PRIM.

Good lack! Thinkest thou so?

MRS. LOVELY (*aside*).

I must second him.— [*Aloud.*] What meaneth this 340 struggling within me? I feel the spirit resisting the vanities of this world, but the flesh is rebellious, yea, the flesh—I greatly fear the flesh, and the weakness thereof—hum—

323. here will] *D1*; there will *D2*.

---

327. *'Sdeath*] *obs.*, except as interjection, contraction for "God's death."
339. *Good lack*] a corruption of "God lack," *obs.*, for "God alack," exclamation of dismay, "God pity that it should be so."

PRIM.

The maid is inspired.

COLONEL.

Behold, her light begins to shine forth.— (*Aside.*)   Excel- 345
lent woman.

MRS. LOVELY.

This good man hath spoken comfort unto me, yea, comfort,
I say; because the words which he hath breathed into my
outward ears are gone through and fixed in mine heart, yea,
verily in mine heart, I say—and I feel the spirit doth love 350
him exceedingly, hum—

COLONEL (*aside*).

She acts it to the life.

Enter Mrs. Prim.

PRIM.

Prodigious! The damsel is filled with the spirit, Sarah.

MRS. PRIM.

I am greatly rejoiced to see such a change in our beloved
Ann. —I came to tell thee that supper stayeth for thee.   355

COLONEL.

I am not disposed for thy food; my spirit longeth for more
delicious meat. Fain would I redeem this maiden from the
tribe of sinners and break those cords asunder wherewith
she is bound—hum—

MRS. LOVELY.

Something whispers in my ears, methinks, that I must be 360
subject to the will of this good man and from him only must
hope for consolation—hum—it also telleth me that I
am a chosen vessel to raise up seed to the faithful and that
thou must consent that we two be one flesh according to
the Word—hum—   365

PRIM.

What a revelation is here! This is certainly part of thy
vision, friend; this is the maiden's growing to thy side.
Ah, with what willingness should I give thee my consent,
could I give thee her fortune too; but thou will never
get the consent of the wicked ones.   370

352.1. *Enter* Mrs. Prim] *follows l.*
353 in D1 and D2.

COLONEL (*aside*).

My I wish I was as sure of yours.

PRIM [*to* Mrs. Lovely].

My soul rejoiceth, yea, it rejoiceth, I say, to find the
spirit within thee; for lo, it moveth thee with natural
agitation—yea, with natural agitation, I say again, and
stirreth up the seeds of thy virgin inclination towards 375
this good man—yea, it stirreth, as one may say, yea,
verily, I say, it stirreth up thy inclination—yea, as one would
stir a pudding.

MRS. LOVELY.

I see, I see—the spirit guiding of thy hand, good Obadiah
Prim, and now behold thou art signing thy consent. —And 380
now I see myself within thy arms, my friend and brother,
yea, I am become bone of thy bone and flesh of thy flesh
(*embraces him*)—hum—

COLONEL (*aside*).

Admirably performed.— [*Aloud.*]   And I will take thee
in all spiritual love for an helpmeet, yea, for the wife of 385
my bosom. —And now, methinks, I feel a longing—yea, a
longing, I say, for the consummation of thy love, hum—yea,
I do long exceedingly.

MRS. LOVELY.

And verily, verily, my spirit feeleth the same longing.

MRS. PRIM.

The spirit hath greatly moved them both. Friend Prim, 390
thou must consent; there is no resisting of the spirit.

PRIM.

Yea, the light within showeth me that I shall fight a good
fight, and wrestle through those reprobate fiends, thy other
guardians—yea, I perceive the spirit will hedge thee into
the flock of the righteous—thou art a chosen lamb—yea, 395
a chosen lamb, and I will not push thee back—no, I will
not, I say, no, thou shalt leap-a and frisk-a and skip-a and

385. helpmeet] helpmete *D1*; help-   387. hum] *D1*; *omitted in D2.*
mate *D2*.

385. *helpmeet*] helpmate; erroneously formed by taking "help meet
[proper]" (Genesis 2:18) as a compound; rarely used as a single, un-
hyphenated word in the early eighteenth century.

bound, and bound, I say—yea, bound within the fold
of the righteous—yea, even within thy fold, my brother.
—Fetch me the pen and ink, Sarah, and my hand shall 400
confess its obedience to the spirit.   [*Exit* Mrs. Prim.]

COLONEL [*aside*].

I wish it were over.

Enter Mrs. Prim *with pen and ink.*

MRS. LOVELY (*aside*).

I tremble lest this Quaking rogue should return and spoil
all.

PRIM.

Here, friend, do thou write what the spirit prompteth, 405
and I will sign it.   Colonel *sits down.*

MRS. PRIM.

Verily, Ann, it greatly rejoiceth me to see thee reformed
from that original wickedness wherein I found thee.

MRS. LOVELY.

I do believe thou art, and I thank thee.

COLONEL (*reads* [*aloud*]).

"This is to certify all whom it may concern that I do freely 410
give up all my right and title in Ann Lovely to Simon
Pure and my full consent that she shall become his wife,
according to the form of marriage. Witness my hand."

PRIM.

That is enough. Give me the pen.   *Signs it.*

Enter Betty, *running to* Mrs. Lovely.

BETTY.

O, madam, madam, here's the Quaking man again; he 415
has brought a coachman and two or three more.

MRS. LOVELY (*aside to* Colonel).

Ruined past redemption.

COLONEL [*aside to* Mrs. Lovely].

No, no, one minute sooner had spoiled all, but now—
[*aloud*] here is company coming, friend; give me the
paper.   *Going up to* Prim *hastily.* 420

403. lest] *D2*; least *D1*.

PRIM.

Here it is, Simon, and I wish thee happy with the maiden.

MRS. LOVELY.

'Tis done, and now, devil do thy worst.

Enter Simon Pure *and* Coachman, *etc.*

PURE.

Look thee, friend, I have brought these people to satisfy
thee that I am not that impostor which thou didst take me
for; this is the man which did drive the leathern con- 425
veniency that brought me from Bristol, and this is

COLONEL.

Look ye, friend, to save the court the trouble of examining
witnesses, I plead guilty, ha, ha.

PRIM.

How's this? Is not thy name Pure, then?

COLONEL.

No, really, sir, I only made bold with this gentleman's name. 430
But I here give it up safe and sound; it has done the business
which I had occasion for, and now I intend to wear my
own, which shall be at his service upon the same occasion
at any time, ha, ha, ha.

PURE.

O, the wickedness of this age.   435

COACHMAN [*to* S. Pure].

Then you have no farther need of us, sir.   *Exeunt.*

COLONEL.

No, honest man, you may go about your business.

PRIM.

I am struck dumb with thy impudence, Ann; thou hast
deceived me and perchance undone thyself.

MRS. PRIM.

Thou art a dissembling baggage, and shame will overtake 440
thee.   *Exit.*

PURE.

I am grieved to see thy wife so much troubled; I will
follow and console her.   *Exit.*

---

424. didst] didest *D1–2*.   436. S.D. *Exeunt*] *Exit D1–2*.
425. man which] *D1*; man that *D2*.

Enter Servant.

SERVANT.

Thy brother guardians inquireth for thee; there is another
man with them.   [*Exit.*] 445

MRS. LOVELY (*to the* Colonel).

Who can that other man be?

COLONEL [*aside to* Mrs. Lovely].

'Tis one Freeman, a friend of mine, whom I ordered to
bring the rest of thy guardians here.

Enter Sir Philip, Tradelove, Periwinkle, *and* Freeman.

FREEMAN (*to the* Colonel).

Is all safe? Did my letter do you service?

COLONEL (*aside* [*to* Freeman]).

All, all's safe; ample service.   450

SIR PHILIP.

Miss Nancy, how dost do, child?

MRS. LOVELY.

Don't call me miss, Friend Philip; my name is Ann, thou
knowest.

SIR PHILIP.

What, is the girl metamorphosed?

MRS. LOVELY.

I wish thou wert so metamorphosed. Ah, Philip, throw off 455
that gaudy attire and wear the clothes becoming of thy age.

PRIM (*aside*).

I am ashamed to see these men.

SIR PHILIP.

My age! The woman is possessed.

COLONEL.

No, thou art possessed rather, friend.

TRADELOVE.

Hark ye, Mrs. Lovely, one word with you.   460

                                 Takes hold of her hand.

COLONEL.

This maiden is my wife, thanks to Friend Prim, and thou
hast no business with her.   *Takes her from him.*

TRADELOVE.

His wife! Hark ye, Mr. Freeman.

PERIWINKLE.

Why, you have made a very fine piece of work of it, Mr. Prim.

SIR PHILIP.

Married to a Quaker! Thou art a fine fellow to be left 465
guardian to an orphan, truly. There's a husband for a
young lady.

COLONEL.

When I have put on my beau clothes, Sir Philip, you'll
like me better.

SIR PHILIP.

Thou wilt make a very scurvy beau, friend.   470

COLONEL.

I believe I can prove it under your hand that you thought
me a very fine gentleman in the Park today, about thirty-
six minutes after eleven. Will you take a pinch, Sir Philip,
out of the finest snuffbox you ever saw?

Offers him snuff.

SIR PHILIP.

Ha, ha, ha, I am overjoyed, faith I am, if thou be'st that 475
gentleman. I own I did give my consent to the gentleman I brought here today, but if this is he, I can't be
positive.

PRIM.

Canst thou not? Now, I think thou art a fine fellow to be left
guardian to an orphan—thou shallow-brained shuttle-cock; 480
he may be a pickpocket for aught thou dost know.

PERIWINKLE.

You would have been two rare fellows to have been trusted
with the sole management of her fortune, would ye not,
think ye? But Mr. Tradelove and myself shall take care
of her portion.   485

TRADELOVE.

Ay, ay, so we will. —Did not you tell me the Dutch merchant
desired me to meet him here, Mr. Freeman?

FREEMAN.

I did so, and I am sure he will be here, if you'll have a
little patience.

475. that] *D1*; the *D2*.

COLONEL.

What, is Mr. Tradelove impatient; nay then, ik ben gereet 490
voor you; heb ye Jan van Timtamtirelireletta Heer van
Fainwell vergeeten?

TRADELOVE.

O, pox of the name! What, have you tricked me too, Mr.
Freeman?

COLONEL.

Tricked, Mr. Tradelove! Did I not give you two thousand 495
pound for your consent fairly? And now do you tell a
gentleman that he has tricked you?

PERIWINKLE.

So, so, you are a pretty guardian, faith; sell your charge!
What did you look upon her as, part of your stock?

PRIM.

Ha, ha, ha! I am glad thy knavery is found out, however. 500
I confess the maiden overreached me and no sinister end at
all.

PERIWINKLE.

Ay, ay, one thing or another overreached you all; but I'll
take care he shall never finger a penny of her money, I
warrant you—overreached, quoth'a? Why, I might have 505
been overreached too, if I had had no more wit. I don't
know but this very fellow may be him that was directed to
me from Grand Cairo today. Ha, ha, ha.

COLONEL.

The very same, sir.

PERIWINKLE.

Are you so, sir? But your trick would not pass upon me. 510

COLONEL.

No, as you say, at that time it did not; that was not my
lucky hour. But hark ye, sir, I must let you into one secret.
You may keep honest John Tradescant's coat on, for
your uncle, Sir Toby Periwinkle, is not dead; so the charge
of mourning will be saved, ha, ha. Don't you remember 515
Mr. Pillage, your uncle's steward, ha, ha, ha?

497. gentleman] gentlemen *D1–2*.

490–492. *ik . . . vergeeten*] I will be ready for you. Have you forgotten
Jan . . .

PERIWINKLE.

Not dead! I begin to fear I am tricked too.

COLONEL.

Don't you remember the signing of a lease, Mr. Periwinkle?

PERIWINKLE.

Well, and what signifies that lease, if my uncle is not dead?
Ha! I am sure it was a lease I signed—   520

COLONEL.

Ay, but it was a lease for life, sir, and of this beautiful
tenement, I thank you.

Taking hold of Mrs. Lovely.

OMNES.

Ha, ha, ha, neighbor's fare!

FREEMAN.

So, then, I find you are all tricked, ha, ha.

PERIWINKLE.

I am certain I read as plain a lease as ever I read in my   525
life.

COLONEL.

You read a lease, I grant you, but you signed this contract.

Showing a paper.

PERIWINKLE.

How durst you put this trick upon me, Mr. Freeman; did
not you tell me my uncle was dying?

FREEMAN.

And would tell you twice as much to serve my friend, ha,   530
ha.

SIR PHILIP.

What, the learned, famous Mr. Periwinkle choused, too, ha,
ha, ha. I shall die with laughing, ha, ha, ha.

PRIM.

It had been well if her father had left her to wiser heads
than thine and mine, friend, ha, ha.   535

TRADELOVE.

Well, since you have outwitted us all, pray you, what and
who are you, sir?

---

523. *neighbor's fare*] *fig.*, and proverbial, connoting a comfortable condition.

SIR PHILIP.

Sir, the gentleman is a fine gentleman. —I am glad you
have got a person, madam, who understands dress and good
breeding. —I was resolved she should have a husband of my 540
choosing.

PRIM.

I am sorry the maiden is fallen into such hands.

TRADELOVE.

A beau! Nay, then she is finely helped up.

MRS. LOVELY.

Why, beaus are great encouragers of trade, sir, ha, ha.

COLONEL.

Look ye, gentlemen, I am the person who can give the 545
best account of myself, and I must beg Sir Philip's pardon
when I tell him that I have as much aversion to what
he calls dress and breeding as I have to the enemies of
my religion. I have had the honor to serve his Majesty and
headed a regiment of the bravest fellows that ever pushed 550
bayonet in the throat of a Frenchman; and notwith-
standing the fortune this lady brings me, whenever my
country wants my aid, this sword and arm are at her
service.

> And now, my fair, if you'll but deign to smile,   555
> I meet a recompense for all my toil.
> Love and religion ne'er admit restraint,
> Force makes many a sinner, not one saint;
> Still free as air the active mind does rove,
> And searches proper objects for its love;   560
> But that once fixed, 'tis past the power of art,
> To chase the dear ideas from the heart.
> 'Tis liberty of choice that sweetens life,
> Makes the glad husband, and the happy wife.

548. calls] *D2*; call's *D1*.

EPILOGUE

Written by Mr. Sewell and Spoken by Mrs. Bullock

What new strange ways our modern beaus devise!
What trials of love skill to gain the prize!
The heathen gods, who never mattered rapes,
Scarce wore such strange variety of shapes.
The devil take their odious barren skulls,   5
To court in form of snakes and filthy bulls.
Old Jove once nicked it, I am told,
In a whole lapful of true standard gold;
How must his godship then fair Danaë warm?
In trucking ware for ware there is no harm.   10
Well, after all—that money has a charm.
But now indeed that stale invention's past;
Besides, you know that guineas fall so fast,
Poor nymph must come to pocket piece at last.
Old Harry's face, or good Queen Bess's ruff—   15
Not that I'd take 'em—may do well enough;
No—my ambitious spirit's far above
Those little tricks of mercenary love.
That man be mine, who, like the Colonel here,
Can top his character in every sphere;   20
Who can a thousand ways employ his wit,
Outpromise statesmen, and outcheat a cit;
Beyond the colors of a trav'ler paint,

In D1, the Epilogue follows the Pro-   in D1.
logue; in D2, the Epilogue follows Act   and Spoken] *D1;* Spoken *D2.*
V and concludes "FINIS," *as does Act V*   9. Danaë] *D2;* Daëne *D1.*

0.2. *Mr. Sewell*] Mrs. Centlivre's good friend Dr. George Sewell (d. 1726), a writer and physician.
7. *nicked it*] hit the mark.
7–9. *Old . . . warm*] The myth of Danaë was used to refer to prostitution.
13. *guineas . . . fast*] In December, 1717, the guinea had been devaluated.
14. *nymph*] euphemistic here: prostitute.
14. *pocket piece*] a coin carried as a charm, often damaged or not current. Widespread clipping of guineas had depreciated their value as bullion.
15–16. *Old . . . enough*] Coins were embossed with the reigning monarch's portrait. Guineas had first been minted in 1663; earlier coins, pocket pieces, might be considered as valuable as clipped or devaluated guineas.

And cant, and ogle too—beyond a saint.
The last disguise most pleased me, I confess;   25
There's something tempting in the preaching dress;
And pleased me more than once a dame of note,
Who loved her husband in his footman's coat.
To see one eye in wanton motions played,
Th'other to the heavenly regions strayed,   30
As if it for its fellow's frailties prayed.
But yet I hope, for all that I have said,
To find my spouse a man of war in bed.

27–28. *And . . . coat*] perhaps a reference to *Three Hours After Marriage*;
Fossile dons his footman's coat to intercept love letters addressed to his wife.

Appendix

Chronology

Approximate years are indicated by *, occurrences in doubt by (?). Dates for plays are those on which they were first made public, either on stage or in print.

Political and Literary Events	*Life and Major Works of Mrs. Centlivre*

1631
Death of Donne.
John Dryden born.

1633
Samuel Pepys born.

1635
Sir George Etherege born.*

1640
Aphra Behn born.*

1641
William Wycherley born.*

1642
First Civil War began (ended 1646).
Theaters closed by Parliament.
Thomas Shadwell born.*

1648
Second Civil War.
Nathaniel Lee born.*

1649
Execution of Charles I.

1650
Jeremy Collier born.

1651
Hobbes' *Leviathan* published.

1652
First Dutch War began (ended 1654).

Thomas Otway born.

1656

D'Avenant's *THE SIEGE OF RHODES* performed at Rutland House.

1657

John Dennis born.

1658

Death of Oliver Cromwell.

D'Avenant's *THE CRUELTY OF THE SPANIARDS IN PERU* performed at the Cockpit.

1660

Restoration of Charles II.

Theatrical patents granted to Thomas Killigrew and Sir William D'Avenant, authorizing them to form, respectively, the King's and the Duke of York's Companies.

Pepys began his diary.

1661

Cowley's *THE CUTTER OF COLEMAN STREET*.

D'Avenant's *THE SIEGE OF RHODES* (expanded to two parts).

1662

Charter granted to the Royal Society.

1663

Dryden's *THE WILD GALLANT*.

Tuke's *THE ADVENTURES OF FIVE HOURS*.

1664

Sir John Vanbrugh born.

Dryden's *THE RIVAL LADIES*.

Dryden and Howard's *THE INDIAN QUEEN*.

Etherege's *THE COMICAL REVENGE*.

1665

Second Dutch War began (ended 1667).

Great Plague.
Dryden's *THE INDIAN EM-
PEROR.*
Orrery's *MUSTAPHA.*

1666
Fire of London.
Death of James Shirley.

1667
Jonathan Swift born.
Milton's *Paradise Lost* published.
Sprat's *The History of the Royal
Society* published.
Shadwell's *THE SULLEN
LOVERS.*

1669
Pepys terminated his diary.   Born in or near Holbeach, Lincoln-
                                              shire.

1670
William Congreve born.
Dryden's *THE CONQUEST OF
GRANADA*, Part I.

1671
Dorset Garden Theatre (Duke's
Company) opened.
Colley Cibber born.
Milton's *Paradise Regained* and
Samson Agonistes published.
Dryden's *THE CONQUEST OF
GRANADA*, Part II.
THE REHEARSAL, by the Duke
of Buckingham and others.
Wycherley's *LOVE IN A WOOD.*

1672
Third Dutch War began (ended
1674).
Joseph Addison born.
Richard Steele born.
Dryden's *MARRIAGE A LA
MODE.*

1674
New Drury Lane Theatre (King's
Company) opened.

Death of Milton.

Nicholas Rowe born.

Thomas Rymer's *Reflections on Aristotle's Treatise of Poesy* (translation of Rapin) published.

1675

Dryden's *AURENG-ZEBE.*

Wycherley's *THE COUNTRY WIFE.**

1676

Etherege's *THE MAN OF MODE*

Otway's *DON CARLOS.*

Shadwell's *THE VIRTUOSO.*

Wycherley's *THE PLAIN DEALER.*

1677

Rymer's *Tragedies of the Last Age Considered* published.

Aphra Behn's *THE ROVER.*

Dryden's *ALL FOR LOVE.*

Lee's *THE RIVAL QUEENS.*

1678

Popish Plot.

George Farquhar born.

Bunyan's *Pilgrim's Progress* (Part I) published.

1679

Exclusion Bill introduced.

Death of Thomas Hobbes.

Death of Roger Boyle, Earl of Orrery.

Charles Johnson born.

1680

Death of Samuel Butler.

Death of John Wilmot, Earl of Rochester.

Dryden's *THE SPANISH FRIAR.*

Lee's *LUCIUS JUNIUS BRUTUS.*

Otway's *THE ORPHAN.*

1681

Charles II dissolved Parliament at Oxford.

Dryden's *Absalom and Achitophel* published.
Tate's adaptation of *KING LEAR.*

1682
The King's and the Duke of York's Companies merged into the United Company.
Dryden's *The Medal, MacFlecknoe,* and *Religio Laici* published.
Otway's *VENICE PRESERVED.*

1683
Rye House Plot.
Death of Thomas Killigrew.
Crowne's *CITY POLITIQUES.*

1684

Married the nephew of Sir Stephen Fox, who died about one year later (?).*

1685
Death of Charles II; accession of James II.
Revocation of the Edict of Nantes.
The Duke of Monmouth's Rebellion.
Death of Otway.
John Gay born.
Crowne's *SIR COURTLY NICE.*
Dryden's *ALBION AND ALBANIUS.*

Married a Captain Carroll, who died about one year later (?).*
Known as Mrs. Carroll in her early works. (May have remarried before 1700.)

1687
Death of the Duke of Buckingham.
Dryden's *The Hind and the Panther* published.
Newton's *Principia* published.

1688
The Revolution.
Alexander Pope born.
Shadwell's *THE SQUIRE OF ALSATIA.*

1689
The War of the League of Augsburg began (ended 1697).

Toleration Act.
Death of Aphra Behn.
Shadwell made Poet Laureate.
Dryden's *DON SEBASTIAN.*
Shadwell's *BURY FAIR.*

1690
Battle of the Boyne.
Locke's *Two Treatises of Government*
and *An Essay Concerning Human
Understanding* published.

1691
Death of Etherege.*
Langbaine's *An Account of the
English Dramatic Poets* published.

1692
Death of Lee.
Death of Shadwell.
Tate made Poet Laureate.

1693
George Lillo born.*
Rymer's *A Short View of Tragedy*
published.
Congreve's *THE OLD BACHELOR.*

1694
Death of Queen Mary.
Southerne's *THE FATAL MAR-
RIAGE.*

1695
Group of actors led by Thomas
Betterton left Drury Lane and
established a new company at
Lincoln's Inn Fields.
Congreve's *LOVE FOR LOVE.*
Southerne's *OROONOKO.*

1696
Cibber's *LOVE'S LAST SHIFT.*
Vanbrugh's *THE RELAPSE.*

1697
Treaty of Ryswick ended the War
of the League of Augsburg.
Charles Macklin born.

Congreve's *THE MOURNING BRIDE.*
Vanburgh's *THE PROVOKED WIFE.*

1698
Collier controversy started with the publication of *A Short View of the Immorality and Profaneness of the English Stage.*

1699
Farquhar's *THE CONSTANT COUPLE.*

1700
Death of Dryden.
Blackmore's *Satire Against Wit* published.
Congreve's *THE WAY OF THE WORLD.*

THE PERJURED HUSBAND, a tragedy, produced at Drury Lane in September.*

1701
Act of Settlement.
War of the Spanish Succession began (ended 1713).
Death of James II.
Rowe's *TAMERLANE.*
Steele's *THE FUNERAL.*

Correspondence with Farquhar published by Abel Boyer in *Letters of Wit, Politics, and Morality.*

1702
Death of William III; accession of Anne.
The Daily Courant began publication.
Cibber's *SHE WOULD AND SHE WOULD NOT.*

THE BEAU'S DUEL: OR, A SOLDIER FOR THE LADIES produced at Lincoln's Inn Fields in June.*
THE STOLEN HEIRESS: OR, THE SALAMANCA DOCTOR OUTPLOTTED produced at Lincoln's Inn Fields in December.

1703
Death of Samuel Pepys.
Rowe's *THE FAIR PENITENT.*

LOVE'S CONTRIVANCE: OR, LE MEDECIN MALGRE LUI produced at Drury Lane in June.
Went to Oxford as a strolling player, an occupation she had, apparently, practiced before (?).

1704

Capture of Gibraltar; Battle of Blenheim.
Defoe's *The Review* began publication (1704–1713).
Swift's *A Tale of a Tub* and *The Battle of the Books* published.
Cibber's *THE CARELESS HUSBAND*.

1705

Haymarket Theatre opened.
Steele's *THE TENDER HUSBAND*

THE GAMESTER produced at Lincoln's Inn Fields in February.
THE BASSET TABLE produced at Drury Lane in November.

1706

Battle of Ramillies.
Farquhar's *THE RECRUITING OFFICER*.

Joined the Duke of Grafton's Servants at Bath. Appeared there in *LOVE AT A VENTURE* (?).*
While a touring actress, met Joseph Centlivre at Windsor.
THE PLATONIC LADY produced at the Haymarket in November.

1707

Union of Scotland and England.
Death of Farquhar.
Henry Fielding born.
Farquhar's *THE BEAUX' STRATAGEM*.

In April, married Centlivre, a cook to Queen Anne who later served George I.

1708

Downes' *Roscius Anglicanus* published.

1709

Samuel Johnson born.
Rowe's edition of Shakespeare published.
The Tatler began publication (1709–1711).

THE BUSY BODY produced at Drury Lane in May; merited Steele's support in *The Tatler*, Nos. 15 and 19.
THE MAN'S BEWITCHED: OR, THE DEVIL TO DO ABOUT HER produced at the Haymarket in December.

1710

A BICKERSTAFF'S BURYING: OR, WORK FOR THE UPHOLD-ERS, a farce, produced at Drury Lane in March.
MAR-PLOT: OR, THE SECOND PART OF THE BUSY BODY produced at Drury Lane in December.

1711
Shaftesbury's *Characteristics* published.
The Spectator began publication (1711–1712).
Pope's *An Essay on Criticism* published.

1712

THE PERPLEXED LOVERS produced at Drury Lane in January. Began a five-year period actively supporting the Whigs, the Protestant Succession, and the Hanovers in her plays and poems.

1713
Treaty of Utrecht ended the War of the Spanish Succession.
Addison's *CATO*.

1714
Death of Anne; accession of George I.
Steele became Governor of Drury Lane.
John Rich assumed management of Lincoln's Inn Fields.
Rowe's *JANE SHORE*.

THE WONDER: A WOMAN KEEPS A SECRET produced at Drury Lane in April; published with a Dedication to the Duke of Cambridge, the future George II.

1715
Jacobite Rebellion.
Death of Tate.
Rowe made Poet Laureate.
Death of Wycherley.

A GOTHAM ELECTION, a farce, published; not acted. Reprinted in 1737 as *THE HUMOURS OF ELECTIONS*.
A WIFE WELL MANAGED, a farce, published; produced at the Haymarket in March, 1724.

1716
Addison's *THE DRUMMER.*

Pope published *A Full and True Account* . . . and *A Further Account* . . . , alluding derisively to Mrs. Centlivre as one of Curll's authors.
THE CRUEL GIFT: OR, THE ROYAL RESENTMENT, a tragedy, produced at Drury Lane in December.

1717
David Garrick born.
Cibber's *THE NON-JUROR.*
Gay, Pope, and Arbuthnot's *THREE HOURS AFTER MARRIAGE.*

1718
Death of Rowe.

A BOLD STROKE FOR A WIFE produced at Lincoln's Inn Fields in February.

1719
Death of Addison.
Defoe's *Robinson Crusoe* published.
Young's *BUSIRIS, KING OF EGYPT.*

1720
South Sea Bubble.
Samuel Foote born.
Steele suspended from the Governorship of Drury Lane (restored 1721).
Little Theatre in the Haymarket opened.
Steele's *The Theatre* (periodical) published.
Hughes' *THE SIEGE OF DAMASCUS.*

1721
Walpole became first Minister.

1722
Steele's *THE CONSCIOUS LOVERS.*

THE ARTIFICE produced at Drury Lane in October.

1723
Death of D'Urfey.

Died on December 1, at her house in Buckingham Court; buried at St. Paul's, Covent Garden.

1725
Pope's edition of Shakespeare published.

1726
Death of Jeremy Collier.
Death of Vanbrugh.
Law's *Unlawfulness of Stage Entertainments* published.
Swift's *Gulliver's Travels* published.

1727
Death of George I; accession of George II.
Death of Sir Isaac Newton.
Arthur Murphy born.

1728
Pope's *The Dunciad* (first version) published.
Cibber's *THE PROVOKED HUSBAND* (expansion of Vanbrugh's fragment *A JOURNEY TO LONDON*).
Gay's *THE BEGGAR'S OPERA*.

1729
Goodman's Fields Theatre opened.
Death of Congreve.
Death of Steele.
Edmund Burke born.

1730
Cibber made Poet Laureate.
Oliver Goldsmith born.
Thomson's *The Seasons* published.
Fielding's *THE AUTHOR'S FARCE*.
Fielding's *TOM THUMB* (revised as *THE TRAGEDY OF TRAGEDIES*, 1731).

1731
Death of Defoe.
Fielding's *THE GRUB-STREET OPERA*.
Lillo's *THE LONDON MERCHANT*.

1732

Covent Garden Theatre opened.

Death of Gay.

George Colman the elder born.

Fielding's *THE COVENT GAR-DEN TRAGEDY*.

Fielding's *THE MODERN HUS-BAND*.

Charles Johnson's *CAELIA*.

1733

Pope's *An Essay on Man* (Epistles I–III) published. (Epistle IV, 1734)

1734

Death of Dennis.

The Prompter began publication (1734–1736).

Theobald's edition of Shakespeare published.

Fielding's *DON QUIXOTE IN ENGLAND*.

1736

Fielding led the "Great Mogul's Company of Comedians" at the Little Theatre in the Haymarket (1736–1737).

Fielding's *PASQUIN*.

Lillo's *FATAL CURIOSITY*.

1737

The Stage Licensing Act.

Dodsley's *THE KING AND THE MILLER OF MANSFIELD*.

Fielding's *THE HISTORICAL REGISTER FOR 1736*.